I AM A TOOL

to help with your dating life

SHELBY ABBOTT

I AM A TOOL, TO HELP WITH YOUR DATING LIFE
Cru Press
100 Lake Hart Drive, Dept. 2500
Orland0, FL 32832-0100

Written by: Shelby Abbott
Edited by: Katie James
Book and Cover Design: Mark Arnold, www.andarnold.com

ISBN 1-57334-095-2

Contents

FORWARD

IT WAS EARLY 2003. There I was sitting in ISAT 2301, a classroom on the campus of James Madison University, listening to a short man talk about dating. He was funny, so I was enjoying myself quite a bit, until he said something that hit me square between the eyes.

Spend less energy on finding the right person and more energy on becoming the right person.

Boom. Wow, I thought. I don't do that. You see, I was your typical girl-crazed college dude. My obsession with humanity's other half wasn't abnormal, I don't think, but it was real. Outwardly I tried to play it cool, of course, but inwardly I was deeply concerned with how I was perceived. I wanted the ladies to notice me, to like me, to admire me, to journal about me.

If you haven't guessed, the short man in the story is Shelby Abbott, and I needed to hear what he said that night at Cru. It was a significant moment for me. I'm a married man with kids but am still thinking about it over a decade later.

Perhaps you know Shelby from conferences like RADIATE and Big Break as the dude up front who makes you laugh. But in his new book, I Am a Tool (To Help with Your Dating Life), the emcee steps off the stage and becomes your friend, offering to help you navigate the tricky waters of lust, longing, and love during the college years.

There's no lack of confusion today about what it means to be men and women. This deep confusion isn't just out there in the culture; it pervades our churches and campus ministries, too. Even if you're not confused, chances are you're unsure—if not downright scared—about the answers to certain questions. What if I'm single and lonely forever? What if no one I like ever likes me back? What if I'm attracted to people of the same sex? How far is too far? Can I do _____ with him, or her? If God wants me to be happy, then why am I so sad? Is singleness a second-rate existence? Do I have to date with the intent to marry? What should I be looking for in a potential spouse anyway?

In chapter after chapter, Shelby takes the questions and fears you can't stop thinking about and holds them up to the bright truth of God's Word. He rightly contends that the ultimate purpose of your singleness, your dating, your marriage—your entire life, in fact—is to honor your Maker and reflect his gospel. If you aren't satisfied in him when you're single, you won't be satisfied in him when you're married. Now is the time to cultivate a lifestyle in which King Jesus is at the center of your solar *system, the gravitational pull holding everything else in orbit.*

Os Guinness has said that the Lord is most against his own gifts when they are put in his place. Think about that. Romantic attraction and dating relationships are good gifts from a good God, but they can easily morph into idols when they're pursued and treasured above him. You will never love another person the right way until you love Jesus more. And that means you haven't found the right person until you've found one who can look at you and say, with honest gladness, you're number two.

I Am a Tool is my friend Shelby at his best. It's witty, winsome, and packed with practical insight from a Christian perspective. Whether your questions or struggles have to do with sex, singleness, DTRs, breakups, or what social media has to do with any of it, Shelby will meet you where you're at and help you move forward in a direction that honors Jesus.

Read this book, but don't do it alone. Invite a friend to go through it with you. Tell an older person in the faith how it's helping and challenging you. And if you're dating, open it up, laugh, learn, and, if necessary, repent.

Friend, do not settle for anything less than a life centered on King Jesus. And when it comes to the complicated arena of dating, let I Am a Tool help show you how.

—Matt Smethurst, Editor at The Gospel Coalition

A hot shower on a cold morning. The latest Hollywood blockbuster movie. Barbecue chicken pizza. Crown molding. Licking your fingers after fifteen minutes of ripping through a bag of Tostito's Hint of Lime tortilla chips. Vin Diesel's voice. The smell of a wood fire in the crisp autumn air. Footsie pajamas for adults.

It can truly be said that all of these things are great things... wonderful things, in fact. Things that can make the corners of your mouth bend upward into a silent, tight smile and fill your heart with sincere happiness. But if you really think about it, these certain some-things that make your life full and glad, none of these can compare to the thrill people experience when they discuss that *one* topic. You know what I'm talking about. Entire magazines, books, television shows, movies, and occupations are devoted to it, and hours of conversation are committed to it on a daily basis. Emotions run high and low because of it, and everyone on the planet has been affected by it in some form or fashion.

If you're honest (and your relationship status happens to be "single"), the subject probably crosses your mind every day...maybe even every hour. In fact, this *one* topic can be the sole filter by which all of your thoughts are siphoned and processed. Obviously, I'm talking about relationships: romance, dating, and the like.

* * *

Every now and then I noodle on little informal social statistical equations in my mind, and I take inventory of what's on the front burner of my life's stove top range, so to speak. I'll be intentional about listening to what the world discusses via advertising, social media, television, radio, casual conversation, and things like that. I want to know what's trending in people's lives.

Sometimes, I'll even make digital tick marks on my smart phone to keep track of things, like how many times food is mentioned in a half hour syndicated sitcom on basic cable TV, or how many times the worship leader at church says "Lord God" when he prays at the end of a three-song set before the pastor gets up to deliver the sermon. Stuff like that.

But the most fun this little game of mine produces is when I start to count the number of times something relationship oriented pops up on the social radar. It's incredible. And because of its frequency, it's nearly impossible to record the number of times people talk about the complexities of dealing with the opposite sex. So much of our world revolves around this subject, and in the ever-changing landscape of what's currently "in," relationships will never, ever go out of fashion.

So I guess the real question is, "What are we to do about it?"

People will always be interested in relationships, and the last time

I checked (which was yesterday, I think), followers of Jesus Christ are people too. Christians tend to be just as obsessed with the opposite gender as anyone else, but the main difference in how we approach this important life subject lies in the specific way we define ourselves. We are Christians, and with that single distinction, the entire topic of relationship is flipped on its head. The standard rules don't apply. Status quo for the way everyone else approaches relationships cannot and should not be the norm for us.

The pages of Scripture call us to something greater and healthier in our relationships with the opposite sex. It calls us to something thrilling and more challenging that involves service, self-sacrifice, communication, and patience.

Sure, anyone can have a relationship, but that doesn't mean that everyone should...especially if the relationship isn't pleasing to God. I've literally seen a 9-year-old boy talk about having lunch with his "girlfriend" at school and how awesome it is because he usually takes and eats her cookies at the end of the lunch period. Unfortunately, such attitudes exist in many places throughout the world – the desire to seek and to take whatever possible for one's own personal benefit in a relationship.

However, as followers of Jesus, we are called to do life differently. It's in our spiritual DNA to be unsettled with the way our culture says that romance should happen. The old has gone and the new has come (2 Cor. 5:17). Therefore, for Christians, it's not "business as usual" when it comes to relationships and dating.

This book is a call for both men and women who love Jesus to drop-kick "business as usual" out the back door. Yes, we will often have relationships on the brain just as much as others, but how we choose to live out those relationships will speak to what and (more importantly) Who we stand for.

SHALL WE DANCE?

But before we dive in here, let me begin by confessing that I will not be writing this book from a position of wisdom gained through great previous successes. What you hold in your hand is by no means a collection of anecdotes on how I got it right, time and time again. I will not be telling you how you should emulate each and every dating practice I lived out over my single years, because the truth is that when I was in the thick of it all, I got it wrong most of the time. My mistakes were plentiful, embarrassing, and sometimes more public than I wanted them to be. However, as a direct result of me getting it wrong, I believe that you could possibly get it right. In other words, you have an opportunity to learn from my mistakes, and that kind of information can be quite valuable if it's put to good use...kind of like a tool.

Tools are instruments that, when used appropriately, can create something quite beautiful. They help us get things done with excellence, and they prevent us from getting hurt in the process. They also help us to avoid wasting time, wasting energy, and wasting our patience. Tools can be glorious things if we choose to utilize them, so consider this book a tool. Yes, you can also think of me as a tool (implication intended), but let's get past all of that and focus on the greater picture of where this tool can lead you.

My goal here is to help guide you through the precarious topic of dating en route God-glorifying relationships with the opposite sex. Sound like an adventure? Well it is, but let me tell you that even though you might think there is some "magic bullet" solution to your specific relationship (or non-relationship) issue, I'm sad to say there isn't. Dealing well with the opposite sex isn't a science. You cannot plug-in and play the same formula for everyone's story and expect it all to work out the exact way you imagine. It isn't static, predictable, easy, or analytical. It's not a science; dating is an art—a dance.

Now, even if the dance metaphor doesn't resonate with you, just go with me on this. You can learn the steps of a dance from watching a video, or you can read up on the appropriate steps, but when it comes time to hit the dance floor, you simply have to feel the music and dance with your partner. You might be scared, you might be off-beat, you might step on the other person's toes, you might trip and stumble in the middle of the dance floor, but in the end, the dance itself is always exhilarating. Conversely, science is safe and practical and precise and people don't usually trip over their feet in the lab, but dance can only be experienced in the raw environment of the real world.

I can try to help you by providing the scientific do's and don'ts of dating and relationships (and I *will* try), but in the end, you're just going to have to feel the music and dance. Study the tools and prepare yourself as a mature, responsible, thoughtful, and caring person, but know that the whole thing can get messy and awkward when the music starts. Lord knows I've stepped on toes and feet and flattened arches in the process of trying to dance well in the world of dating, and my guess is that you will too. But that's okay. Just roll with it.

Oh...you hear that? I think they just started playing your song...

WHAT WE TALK ABOUT
WHEN WE TALK ABOUT DATING

WHY DATING IN THE FIRST PLACE?

It's probably important that we first address the looming question of *why dating and not some other option?* Is dating really the right way to go about pursuing a relationship with the opposite sex? What about courtship? What about just casual hangouts without such an official label as "dating?"

The thing is, when it comes to relationships with the opposite sex in the context of our faith, certain issues aren't always a matter of right or wrong. Sometimes, they are a matter of what is wise or unwise based upon the situation. And, what might be right for one couple may not necessarily be what you feel called to or comfortable with in your own relationships.

I've overheard many sincere advice-givers label specific dating practices as "sinful" or "unbiblical," hoping to shepherd an ignorant advice-seeker toward a more godly relationship. And while the advice-giver's heart is probably in the right place, calling something in the realm of dating "biblical" or "unbiblical" is like saying, "heating your home with electricity is more biblical than heating it with propane gas."

The Bible doesn't say anything in particular about how one should heat his or her home. However, if I were to come over to your place and notice you warm your house by setting little baby chinchillas on fire, I'd have a problem with that. In other words, biblical principles and biblical thinking can be applied to practices that Scripture is silent on. As we get into dating, I'm going to be advocating principles consistent with biblical values, such as valuing and honoring others, being truthful, and communicating openly. Scripture is quite clear on all of these things. We simply need to apply them to the context of dating.

So, even though the Bible has a whole lot of nothin' to say about the American cultural practice of dating—because it didn't exist in biblical times—we can certainly say that dating is not wrong if it's done right. If dating is done well in a biblically influenced, God-honoring way, then it's just the opposite of wrong; it's actually quite appropriate, godly, and fun!

There is, however, plenty of room for sin to creep in and start to transform godly intentions into something that does not honor the Lord, and we'll address this in the coming chapters, but for now, my guess is that dating is currently the most common form of familiarizing oneself with the opposite sex. That is the well-journeyed road I chose to travel when I was single, and it's what I know from my many years of working with college students in full-time missionary work, so I'm going to concentrate on what is likely the most common practice in our culture. People are dating, so let's talk about dating.

But what is *dating* exactly?

DATING DEFINED...SORT OF

The word *dating* might mean totally different things to different people, based on past experiences, books read, information gathered, or lessons learned. Therefore, it is important that I give clear definition to what I'm referring to when I use the term *dating*.

So, what *are* we talking about? Well, I once heard by someone that dating can be conceptualized in terms of the breakdown of the letters within the actual word "date." D.A.T.E. A date should be a Divine Appointment To Encourage. Basically, it's a God-given opportunity to spend time with someone you like, and encourage him or her in the process.

To be honest, when this certain someone told me that a date was a divine appointment to encourage, my first thought was that this guy did not have many appointments to encourage, either regularly or divinely. The pithy cuteness of his definition made me want to roll my eyes and say, "Thanks, but I'll be handling the whole dating-a-lady-thing on my own."

But as time went by, I understood more what he was getting at. To him, a date is an opportunity to show a Christian woman that she is worth spending time, energy, and money on. It is a chance to build-up a sister in Christ, and communicate to her that she is valuable. He enjoys the window of opportunity to encourage a woman, because to him, it is a casual way for a Christian guy to uplift a Christian girl. In his case, however, things didn't ever seem to move past that casual date phase into something deeper. So, while I agree with the concept of the D.A.T.E. paradigm, for me it seems to lean a little toward care-free or indifferent.

Yes, of course it's important to encourage the other person while on a date and communicate care via time, energy, forethought, and money on something like dinner. I absolutely agree. But the non-committal attitude can actually cause more harm than good without healthy communication before, during, and after the date about each person's intentions. This constant defining and redefining can be exhausting and awkward. Plus, this guy friend of mine began to acquire a reputation as a player with the ladies, so his strategy toward dating, no matter how sincere he was with his intentions, ended up coming back around to bite him in the rear-end after all was said and done.

Yes, I agree that dating can and should be a series of divine appointments to encourage someone, but I'd like to add a bit more to the definition and say that dating should not just be about the dates. When you are dating someone, there should be a standard for clear communication about what's actually going on between the two of you. Are you dating exclusively? Are you ready to attach the label of "boyfriend or girlfriend?" Is this moving toward something more serious? These kinds of questions shouldn't constantly be looming in the minds and hearts of the two people who are dating one another, and the remedy for chronic questioning is communication. Both of the people going out on this series of dates should understand with clarity the intentions of the other and the direction in which the relationship is headed.

So, to wrap it up in one sentence, here's my definition of dating: A series of divine appointments to encourage the other person with the assumption that the God-honoring relationship is clearly defined via healthy and appropriate communication.

JUST HANGING OUT

That, in a sentence or two, is what I mean by dating—what I think Christian dating looks like. And maybe just as important to clarify, here's what I think it should *not* look like. As Christians, we allow culture to define who we are and how we behave in our everyday lives way too often. This is especially true when it comes to the practice of relating to the opposite sex. What is widely accepted as standard or "normal" in the dating world at large, sadly becomes the standard for Christians as well.

According to a recent *New York Times article*[1], many young singles are now in the practice of living inside a "dating culture [that] has evolved into a cycle of text messages." Because we live and breathe and hide behind our phones, the non-committal "whatever" attitude in culture has downgraded this opportunity for encouragement into something referred to as, "one step below dating and one step above high-fiving."

The article goes on to say, "Dinner at a romantic new bistro? Forget it. Women in their 20s these days are lucky to get a last-minute text to tag along. Raised in the age of so-called 'hookup culture,' [young people] — who are reaching an age where they are starting to think about settling down — are subverting the rules of courtship. Instead of dinner-and-a-movie, which seems as obsolete as a rotary phone, they rendezvous over phone texts, Facebook posts, instant messages and other 'non-dates' that are leaving a generation confused about how to land a boyfriend or girlfriend."[2]

This is from the *New York Times*, but as I stand back and observe what's going on inside the Christian culture, I'm quickly realizing that we're simply playing copy-cat. For Christians, the new idea behind dating is just "hanging out": a safe, comfortable, and to be honest, lazy way to approach the dating scene. It reinforces an already existing improper urge to extend adolescence beyond what it should be.

Whatever. We're not dating. She's not my girlfriend or anything... we're just hanging out. Why should I have to label it?

Boyfriend? No, he's not my boyfriend. He's just a guy I hang out with all the time...he's like a really good friend that happens to be a guy, but we're not a couple or anything.

These are childish, vague words and phrases spoken by immature people who would rather give more commitment to a video game or cell phone than a sister or brother in Christ who deserves to be treated with enough respect to be communicated with appropriately.

Simply put, "hanging out" is not dating, even if two people are hanging out every night of every week. Dating should not be casual or ambiguous or "whatever." It should be intentional, communicative, and approached with initiative. If someone asks you what is going on with the guy or girl you've been hanging out with on a regular basis, you should be able to give clear definition and never once have to shrug your shoulders. The world is telling you to hide behind a text message because it's easier that way, and you won't have to put your heart out there and get hurt. That's just a silly way to protect yourself from being rejected, and it's not really showing honor to God. Oh, and there's something else that I would not define as dating...

THE BUFFET APPROACH

People are pretty split on the idea of the all-you-can-eat buffet: some love it, some gag at the thought. But as a general demographic, I think it's safe to say that most American college males love the concept.

"Pay one low price and get to eat all you want? How on earth could this be considered anything but amazing?" says the dude. However, there are many people in society who would rather eat at a gas station on their birthday than pay good money to eat from what I sometimes call a "trough of poorly prepared, poorly warmed, bland tasting slop for the masses."

No matter your view on the American buffet, if you choose to eat at one, the ritual is always the same: grab a dish, roam around a room full of food choices, select what you'd like from behind the glass sneeze guard, spoon it onto your plate, sit down at your table, eat as much of it as you want, and then go back and get more. Repeat as many times as your stomach can handle, and finish with a bowl of banana pudding or a chocolate/vanilla twisty cone from the self-serve ice cream machine.

Well, whether you love or hate standing at a public feeding trough and shoveling "nutrition"onto your platter, the idea of a "buffet" should remain solely in the culinary world, never creeping into the world of dating. And here's what I mean...

There are people who treat dating as if they are roaming around an environment, selecting someone, consuming what they want from that person, throwing the relationship away, and quickly moving on to the next person. Or, they take a little bit of something from one person at the same time they are trying out another, without any real sense of maturity, relational health, communication, or commitment. They treat the opposite sex as something they casually select for their own personal satisfaction, and if they don't like the taste, they quickly discard it in order to move on to someone else. With this kind of carelessness, people can get very, very hurt.

The "buffet approach" is not acceptable when it comes to dating. Those who characterize dating in a way that treats others like a side dish to be sampled and discarded are not at all on the same page as me or what I mean by the term *dating*. The world may accept relationship hopping and sampling multiple partners at once. I do not.

Dating with the buffet approach is the epitome of self-serving and is therefore not at all a part of my definition.

WHAT ARE YOU SAYING?

So, let's step back and again go over what I'm saying and what I'm not saying when I talk about dating. I mentioned earlier that dating is a series of divine appointments to encourage, under the assumption that the God-honoring relationship is clearly defined through healthy and appropriate communication. That's what I believe dating should be.

Since dating can be such an ambiguous notion, I feel like it is of great importance that we are all thinking through the same grid before we began to tackle the more intricate details of a relationship.

And now that we've built the foundation, let's get into the nitty-gritty.

WE BELONG TOGETHER

It is not good for man to be alone.
—God

It's no secret that men and women are different from one another. And although you might scoff at me stating that, given the fact that I didn't truly absorb that little gem of information fully until I reached college-age, my bet is that you too sometimes forget it's true. Men are very different from women, and women are quite dissimilar to men.

Generally speaking, women like to smell pretty. Consequently, they will often spend tremendous amounts of money on things that make them smell nice: perfume, pleasant shower gels, fragrant bath oils, and aromatic hand soaps from Bath & Body Works. Girls like to be closely associated to sweet-scented things, such as flowers, cucumbers, and melon. They do...men do not.

Men have absolutely no desire to smell like fruits or vegetables, and they certainly have no urge to smell like fruits and vegetables. Cucumber melon is never a part of the thought process when men wash their hands, because men would much rather smell like dirt or beef or blood. In fact, if you took a poll, my guess is that men would probably be fine with smelling like all three of these things at the same time: dirty, beefy blood.

Back when I was in college, a buddy of mine lived in a co-ed dorm where the men and women were separated by a floor. I remember paying him a visit one time, and as I walked up the stairwell to the fifth floor where he lived, my nose became my guide, and through deductive reasoning, it was pretty easy to know which gender lived on which floor. Climbing the stairs brought with it the scent of feet, then coconut, then stale beer, then cinnamon, then finally gym socks. Conclusion: dudes, ladies, dudes, ladies, dudes.

Men and women are different.

The cool thing is that even through our differences, we still long to be together. Men may roll their eyes at the fact that women are always trying to smell nice (and will go to great lengths to do so), but as we feign exasperation, we are secretly adoring every moment. Women may act disgusted by a guy when he comes home from the gym, covered in sweat and reeking of a locker room, but they are secretly drawn to the raw masculinity that emanates from a man who works out and smells funky.

You know it's true. We repel each other, but we also attract each other.

There are countless other examples of how we do things differently, think in contrasting ways, communicate on different levels, and share differing passions, but the undeniable fact is that we still keep coming back to our hard-wired, God-given desire to be with one another. We belong together.

In Genesis 2:18, God is quoted as saying:

It is not good for the man to be alone. I will make a helper suitable for him.

And the Scripture goes on to say in verse 24:

That is why a man leaves his father and mother and is united to his wife, and they become one flesh.

After this, Genesis records some personal stuff that happens, mostly involving the absence of clothing (if you're super curious, go look it up for yourself). Regardless, we can see very clearly in the Bible that God made men and women with differences, but He also made them for the distinct purpose of uniting. This union serves men and women quite nicely, but it also brings great glory to God in the process. When a man and a woman come together in the covenant commitment of marriage, the union itself forms a bond that is in tune with what the Lord—the good Lord— intended. It hums in perfect pitch, and projects a picture that points to the future joining of Jesus Christ with his bride—the church.

The natural attraction men and women feel for one another is God-designed: it's good, it's right, it's beautiful, and it's healthy. It's meant to be undertaken in the best way possible, via the context of marriage, and the precursor to this union can be experienced in dating. But of course, like every other good thing God created in this world, this attraction and desire to be together has been horribly tainted by sin.

THREE LETTERS: S-E-X

Through many venues and many eager teachers, we receive input on how to live life. Unfortunately, most of these teachers are ill-equipped or just altogether wrong for the job. The world, our sinful nature, and Satan, are quick to speak-up on how you should approach a relationship with the opposite sex, and what you should do with your body sexually during your single years. These teachers are all very excited to go on and on about the topic in great detail, and therein lies our problem.

I don't have any official polling numbers on this, but it's probably safe to say that about ninety nine percent of the input we get on how to date (or how to approach sex) is from a worldly, sinful perspective, and that information is all rather graphic, detailed, and explicit. The input we do get from the Christian community is usually too little, too late, too vague, and too sanitized to be much practical help.

I know what I'm about to say isn't common verbiage from the pulpit on a Sunday morning, but I need to tell you something very important: sex is not a bad thing. Sex is a good thing...a very good thing. Our bodies are good things. They are God's design. He invented them and He also invented sex. It's just really, really sad that we have to learn about it from the world.

Everyone on the planet is interested in sex once they hit a certain age, and what they are learning over and over again from the wrong source is, "The more you practice, the better you get." Because media is fiber-optically streamed directly into homes and even pockets via onscreen entertainment available on cellphones, people are educating themselves about sex under the tutelage of cinematographers, studio executives, cameramen, paid actors, and even pornographers.

In his book *TheoMedia: The Media of God and the Digital Age*, Andrew Byers says, "For Christians anticipating (or trying to enjoy) marital sex for the long haul, considerable unlearning is required."[3] Why? Because we are all being spoon-fed a considerable and consistent string of lies that deceive us into believing things that simply aren't true. The lies are often very clear: sex has no consequence; sex is an end goal, not a beginning; if you're serious about the person you're dating, you should be having sex; there's something seriously wrong with you if you're not sexually active...and it goes on and on.

Yes, sex is a great thing, but it must happen within the proper context in order for it to be experienced in the most exciting, pleasurable, and godly way possible. This reminds me of a former roommate of mine and his pet fish. For the sake of this story, I'll call the fish Albert...but he really didn't have a name.

ONE FISH, TWO FISH, ORANGE FISH, DEAD FISH

Back when I was a single dude living with a few other guys in an apartment, one of my roommates had a medium-sized, twenty-gallon fish tank containing three or four fish. It was positioned in his room right next to his desk. Every now and then I would go into his bedroom to sit in his desk chair and swivel it toward the fish tank to watch the little car key-sized creatures swim around their home. I did this often in order to help myself relax a bit after a long day of work, because watching fish swim can be very therapeutic (that's why you find fish tanks in doctor's offices).

Anyway, one day I found myself sitting in my roommate's chair, staring at one bright orange fish, a.k.a. Albert, as he swam from side-to-side in the tank, nibbling on little black specs of whatever gunk was on the tiny pebbles at the bottom of his home's floor. As I watched him swim and nibble, swim and nibble, swim and nibble, a thought came to my brain that made me take pause.

Why should my roommate's cute little fish be confined to this cramped little tank? It's not very big in there, and he has to share it with two or three other fish for every second of his life. That's not fair! This adorable goldfish should be allowed to experience the freedom of roaming around our entire apartment as much as he wants, without the inhibition of confinement to this measly twenty gallon fish tank!

So as these thoughts went through my head, I immediately decided what I must do to right this situation and give my roommate's fish his freedom. I grabbed the little green net-on-a-metal-stick that my roommate kept on the stand next to the fish tank, dipped the net into the water to hunt for the proper aquatic animal, scooped the bright orange fish up with the net, pulled him out of the watery prison he lived in, flipped the net upside down over the middle of my roommate's bedroom floor, and shouted, "You're free, my little orange friend! Roam unhindered anywhere you'd like because you are no longer a slave to your fish tank!"

When Albert, the little orange goldfish, plopped onto the carpet next to a pair of unwashed socks on my roommate's floor, I watched him wiggle around for a few moments as he opened and closed his mouth. "Go, Albert!" I yelled, "You're free!" But the fish just flopped on the ground in that same spot until it stopped moving many moments later...and died.

Now, before you decide that you hate me because of goldfish cruelty, let me tell you that this little event never actually happened. Sorry to mislead you.

Yes, from time to time I did go sit in my roommate's chair and watch his fish swim around in order to sooth my emotions, but never did I stupidly murder one of his cute little swimming friends. So calm down. I told you this story because of what it has the power to illustrate.

True freedom, vibrancy, and life were found for that little goldfish within the context of the water in that fish tank, and anything outside of that environment brought suffocation, and eventually death. Even though I "freed" Albert, the small orange fish from the "prison" of his habitat where he experienced life, into the "bigger, more exciting space of our apartment," the truth was that what looked like liberation was in fact assassination.

And in a similar way, the world is urging each of us to experience the same kind of sexual "liberation" outside the "prison" or constraint of marriage. "It's not fair!" says culture. "You should be allowed the freedom to sexually roam around as you please, without being confined to the boring cage of marriage! Out here is where real life can be found!" But if sex is taken outside the God-given commitment of marriage, it only leads to destruction and brokenness.

See, sex exclusively within a marriage relationship isn't a prison, it's freedom! Sex within marriage is life! It is the gracious, God-created plan for the maximum experience two people can share because they know that they aren't going anywhere. They know that within their marriage, there isn't any embarrassment or comparison or insecurity. They know that the other person isn't going to grab their clothes and leave in the morning. There is no walk of shame for married couples, because they've committed their lives to one another in every way, not just sexually. Sex in marriage is where life is found, and sex outside of marriage, though it may look like liberation, is in fact, assassination.

SEX AND PAPER PRODUCTS

Those three enemies I mentioned earlier (the world, our sinful nature, and Satan) are professional liars. All they do is lie. The Bible even goes so far as to say that the Devil is the "father of lies," and when he lies he is "speaking his native language" (John 8:44). There is no truth at all in anything our three enemies tell us about how to achieve a healthy sexual relationship, but the astounding thing is that nearly everyone on the planet has bought into those lies.

The Enemy would have you believe that getting married as a virgin is ridiculous because why would you "buy a car without test driving it first?" Why on earth would you walk into marriage without knowing what your partner is like in bed? You don't really even know who they are if you've never had sex with them, right? "You need to have plenty of sexual experiences," says the world, the sinful nature, and the Devil, "then and only then will you have a thriving, intimate relationship with your partner, because practice makes perfect."

No doubt you've heard this perspective, witnessed it in someone close to you, or even bought into it yourself. It's like auto insurance commercials: we are saturated by the message. And the ads, along with the lies, just keep on coming.

But when a bond is made via a sexual experience, it is not something that can be easily removed. Engaging in a sexual act with another person is meant to exist within a committed marriage relationship, and without that proper context, lives can quickly be destroyed.

The world's perspective would have you believe that sex is just a thing that happens between two people for the purpose of experiencing selfish pleasure. Even the phrase, "get some" is intrinsically self-serving. This perspective treats the act of sex like the random placement of a sticky note on any person you want to "get some" from. Stick on someone here, then peel away. If you like that person, stick on them for a bit, then peel away. Stick on the hot person you met at the bar, then peel away in the morning. Stick on the person you've had a crush on, then peel away. "Be a sticky note!"

But the catch is, sex was never created to be a temporary thing. It forms a God-designed bond between a man and woman in a loving, committed marriage that is intended to grow into a stronger relationship over time. Sex is not like a sticky note...it's more like an envelope. I know I'm talking a lot about paper here, but stay with me.

When a sexual attachment is made between two people, it's like an envelope flap being sealed at the opening for the purpose of creating a secure bond. And we all know what happens when an envelope is opened, right? There is permanent damage done when the ripping apart starts. Have you ever tried to use an envelope again after it's been sealed and then opened? It's kind-of pointless to try, isn't it? Why? Because it was meant to be attached only one time.

The sinful perspective would have you believe that sex should be treated as if everyone in the world is a sticky note, but what happens to a sticky note if you stick it on too many things? It eventually loses its stickiness, doesn't it? Sex is not a sticky note-type scenario... it's more like an envelope, meant to be attached only once, without being pulled apart and causing irreparable damage. This is God's will for us and for sex...

> It is God's will that you should be sanctified: that you should avoid sexual immorality; that each of you should learn to control your own body in a way that is holy and honorable, not in passionate lust like the pagans, who do not know God...For God did not call us to be impure, but to live a holy life. Therefore, anyone who rejects this instruction does not reject a human being but God, the very God who gives you his Holy Spirit. (1 Thessalonians 4:3-5, 7-8)

God is brilliant. He has intentionally set things up in order to give us the maximum sexual experience possible, so the less that you do now, the more you end up investing into your future. Yes, godly sexual investing takes an extreme amount of patience, but man, it pays off! And I know this from personal experience.

MY PERSONAL SEXUAL HISTORY

I'm not going to brag here and tell you that I'm awesome because I waited until marriage to have sex, but what I will do is unapologetically explain to you that I'm glad I made the decisions that I did. I got married when I was twenty-nine years old, and I was a virgin when I did so. So was my wife, and I have to tell you that there has *never* been a time in my marriage when I've thought to myself, "I really wish that I had more sexual experiences before I got married." And I have certainly never thought, "I wish that my wife had more experience in the bedroom before she married me."

I praise God all the time that neither my wife nor I knew of the marital sexual experience before we were committed to one another in holy matrimony. And as a result of our choices to stay sexually pure, I've never compared her to anyone from my past, she's never wondered if she was better or worse than one of my old girlfriends, we have never worried about sexually transmitted diseases of any kind, and I've never had a flashback from a previous sexual experience when I've been with my wife. It's beautiful, and I continually give thanks to my Maker that he spared each of us in this way.

I'm explaining this to you for a few reasons. First and foremost, I want God to receive more glory for the great things that He has done in my marriage, both before and after the wedding ceremony. And second, to be honest, there aren't too many stories like this to tell. The stories of defeat far outweigh the stories of chastity, so when there's an opportunity to tell my story and point not to my own righteousness, but to His, I want to do it. Jesus be glorified. Isn't He great? I love that God called me to a life of celibacy until I married my wife. I wouldn't have it any other way, and I can say with absolute certainty that I'm so glad we both waited because she was worth it... and I like to think that I was too.

CROSSING THE LINE

I have known and talked to far too many couples who glorify God in nearly every aspect of their dating relationship but cannot seem to be aligned to His calling in the area of sexual purity. It disqualifies so many potential leaders and destroys opportunities for ministry and mission time and time again. So, if we claim to be followers of Christ, then others must be able to see Jesus in every single aspect of our dating lives. If you were to place your dating relationship up on a pedestal (metaphorically speaking) then Christ should shine brightly and be clearly visible through that relationship from each and every angle.

Opportunities to cross the line will always be plentiful any time you're dating, so it's important to communicate on the front end of any dating relationship what your physical boundaries should be. This way, both of you in the relationship can keep one another accountable regarding the boundaries you've set up. I'd also recommend that whatever boundaries have been put in place, these should be shared with a few close friends — third parties who care about you and your dating relationship. A roommate or best friend or someone you're comfortable being vulnerable with is always a good choice.

What I won't do is tell you the specific physical boundaries you should have in your dating relationship. I refuse to do this because I don't want to unintentionally communicate something that might cause a dating couple to stumble and fall into sin. What might be fine for one pair might be very difficult for another...it totally depends on the boundary lines each couple has formed.

(As an aside, however, if you would like some specific tracks to run on when it comes to boundaries, Betty Blake Churchill has written a wonderful book called *Fantasy*[4] that includes a chapter entitled *I Gave My Word to Stop at Third*. She runs through one couple's specifics about what to do and what not to do in the physical areas of dating, and she unpacks it quite nicely with generous amounts of humor. I'd recommend it.)

I have known friends who didn't even kiss until after they both said "I do" on their wedding. This was their decision, and I respect it with all of my heart. When my wife and I were dating, we were very intentional about communicating with clarity to one another (and some close friends) what our physical boundaries would be, and we kept revisiting that conversation as things became more difficult the longer we were together. I won't lie and tell you that we never crossed the boundary lines we set up, but I will say we were both aware of those lines, and had to be in constant communication with one another about the particulars. In the heat of a romantic moment, one tends to look for loopholes in the boundary specifications...and we were no strangers to this.

Again, we were not perfect, but our boundary lines were set pretty high, so if/when we crossed them, we would confess to our accountability friends, ask forgiveness from the Lord/each other, and we set higher standards for the future. And because our boundaries were set pretty conservatively, when we did stumble, our lives weren't characterized by an overwhelming sense of guilt, remorse, or shame...and we were never driving to the local pharmacy to buy a pregnancy test.

I'm going to double my resolve here and tell you once again that it's important to talk with others when it comes to these kinds of boundaries. An isolated couple is a couple in danger. Now, that may sound stupid because the nature of a couple implies two people and not one, but I think you get what I'm saying when I urge you to involve other God-fearing people you trust in your decision making about physical boundaries. This can only lead to healthy, godly dating relationships and wise decision making.

A PAST YOU'RE NOT PROUD OF

Whenever I end up talking about the subject of sexual purity and the importance of remaining sexually pure in a dating relationship, I inevitably end up getting asked a series of very legitimate follow-up questions about sexual impurity in the past. Anxiety can flood someone's heart when they hear all that I've shared with you thus far, and thoughts somewhere along the lines of, *well, that's great for people who haven't screwed up their past yet, but what about me?*, end up rising to the surface.

Questions like this are valid. If we neglect these kinds of issues and pretend that nobody has ever messed up in the past, we are being obtuse and ignoring a large section of the population who long for answers and the kind of grace that is lavishly poured out on each of us in the truth of the gospel.

Perhaps you have come to know Christ just recently, and you have a sexual history with every person you've ever dated. Or maybe you've been a Christian for quite some time but you were still looking for acceptance and love from a boyfriend or girlfriend in your past, and that led you to some sexual experiences you are now ashamed of. Or, perhaps, this whole concept of sexual purity is brand new to you and the idea of not being sexually intimate with your boyfriend or girlfriend is completely foreign because that's the way you've always been; no one has ever told you anything different. There could be countless reasons for anyone to say, "Well, all that stuff about staying pure is good, and I want to do that from this day forward, but I'll never be able to change my imperfect past."

Maybe you are like Marion Jordan Ellis, who in describing her single years said, "As my partying [lifestyle] accelerated, the fuel light on my soul began to blink a bright orange. Feeling like I was running on empty, and desperate to fill the tank, I cranked up the intake of boys and booze."[5]

So, what about *those* people? Honestly, I'd imagine many of you who are reading this are one of "those people," so first let me say something that I hope will stick with you regardless of what your past may hold: Jesus offers healing.

If we are in Christ, the Bible says we are a new creation (2 Corinthians 5:17). Things that used to be true of us in our history are dead and we are made new and perfect because of Jesus' redeeming work on the cross. In Christ alone is forgiveness, restoration, newness of life, and healing of our past failures. Even if you've messed up in the past after you became a Christian, you are still wholly accepted and made new by the sacrificial blood offering that Jesus made for you when He hung from the tree. You can take comfort and rest in the fact that when God sees you, He does not see your past sexual compromises, but your newness in His Son and the blood that covers your life for all eternity. You are clean in His eyes!

And when it comes down to it, it is only God's opinion that truly counts. We can move forward in our lives with confidence in knowing that the shortcomings of our past in the sexual area do not define us. If we are in Christ, we are all spiritual virgins and the truth of our purity is again a testament to the goodness of God and how glorious He is. I said it before, and I'll say it again: Isn't He great? See, it's not about how great we are or how great we can be from here on out. It's about how amazing He is because of His grace, His love, His sacrifice, and His perfection. If you are a virgin and have never compromised in that area before, praise God for His graciousness in your life! If you have stumbled and crossed the line sexually many times in your past, praise God that He has forgiven you and offers His gracious healing in your life! Either way, God is good and He gets the glory.

It's all about Him.

If you have a past you are not proud of, rejoice in the fact that God has restored you to the new creation you now are. This is your identity, so rest in it and don't believe the lie that you won't be able to climb out of the pit of despair containing your sexually immoral history. Christ's sacrificial blood that buys your forgiveness is bigger than your sordid past.

The children's song that you more than likely know by heart, says it well:

> *Jesus loves me, this I know*
> *For the Bible tells me so*
> *Little ones to Him belong*
> *They are weak, but He is strong*
> *Yes, Jesus loves me*
> *Yes, Jesus loves me*
> *Yes, Jesus loves me*
> *The Bible tells me so.*[6]

Jesus loves you. Yes, He does. Soak it in and live like you believe it because the Bible tells you so.

Amen and amen.

A FIRM FOUNDATION

I'm pretty sure that all of my best thoughts and ideas come to me while I'm mowing my lawn. I can't really prove it, of course, but I'm fairly certain I've been able to solve 93% of the world's problems during the 1.3 hours a week I spend cutting the grass around my house in the summer. Lots of stuff goes through my mind when I push that mower back and forth, so let me share a few examples with you so you can see what I'm talking about:

- I've come up with a better ending to every Nicolas Cage movie I've ever seen.

- I've created the perfect list of things to say to any party host after I've used his bathroom.

- If I could get feral squirrels to obey my every command, I would be able to successfully overthrow the ruling powers at nearly every college campus in America.

- I know exactly what I will say if I'm ever interviewed by Conan O'Brien...and I have the perfect illustration that will lead smoothly into a clear gospel presentation.

Okay, so no, I'm not actually solving any of the world's real problems, but what I think about while I'm mowing the lawn is just the tip of a very large iceberg of thoughts that come to me. By this logic, however, I'm a complete idiot in the winter months when I'm unable to bust out the lawnmower and cut my grass. For some reason, shoveling snow doesn't seem to garner the same type of creative output from my brain. Oh well. I'll just have to settle for the warmer months and label the winter as "hibernation time." If bears do it, I can too.

So what does all of this have to do with dating? I'm glad you asked. My intention here is to try to illustrate that there are seasons in life when things are productive, motivating, energizing, and all around joyful. On the flip side, there are periods of time in life when things just don't go too well. Those seasons can be cumbersome, boring, unproductive, and pretty depressing.

As human beings, we are meant to experience life, and when periods of time come that drain life from us, we instinctively know things aren't good…things are not the way they should be. Jesus said, "I have come that they may have life, and have it to the full" (John 10:10b). By this, we know that the kind of life Jesus desires for His followers isn't a mundane life of boredom, bondage, depression, or "hibernation." The Lord wants life to be joyful, thrilling, creative, zealous, and full of excitement. This includes our interaction with the opposite sex.

(Disclaimer: This is not to say that the Christian life is simply about happiness. We are also called to suffer for the sake of Christ [See 2 Timothy and the like] and expect trials to be a normal part of our lives with God. Abundant life is life connected to Christ and abiding in Him (John 15:4-5), in both the tough times and the joyful times.)

A lot of people have the tendency to think a Christian dating relationship is dull or lacks adventure. And while there may be plenty of examples to feed the stereotype, this doesn't mean that your life needs to be this way. If you're under the impression that Jesus wants you to conform to some ridiculous mold that sucks the fun out of your dating life, it's time to rethink who Jesus is and start to form a renewed mindset about what His desires are for your life. He wants you to enjoy dating to the fullest. He wants you to begin to lay the foundational groundwork now so you can build upon it as time moves forward in your dating relationship.

Shaping that foundation is critical, and there are a few important questions we must ask ourselves before a relationship spontaneously begins to grow. As two people spend time together and a relationship begins to take shape, things can crumble easily if it is not built on a solid and proper foundation. So, what exactly are the important questions to consider?

ARE YOU GOING IN THE SAME DIRECTION?

Imagine for a moment that I'm holding a large rubber band gripped equally between my left and right fists as my knuckles face each other. *Um, what?* Hang with me here, and this will make sense. The rubber band I'm holding between both fists is pliable enough so that I'm able to stretch it with ease as I pull my fists apart, and then bring them back together so that my knuckles touch.

Now, if I were to slowly pull my closed hands apart in opposite directions, still gripping the rubber band between them, I would reach a certain point at which the rubber band would be stretched to its limit. If my fists moved away from one another, the tension would continue to increase and increase until the rubber band would finally reach its breaking point and snap in my hands. Understand?

Good. Now, let me explain to you why I just asked you to imagine that little scenario with me. There comes a point in every dating relationship when the question needs to be asked, "Am I going in the same direction as this person?" Maybe you have a passion for travel and the person you're dating doesn't really like to leave home for longer than a weekend. Well, if the relationship started to get more serious and you began to consider marriage, this could potentially be a pretty big problem.

Maybe you have a desire to go into missions, but the guy you're seriously dating wants to be a business person in the marketplace. He has no desire at all to be a full-time missionary, and you have no desire to have a job that doesn't relate to missions work. Again, this could be a big problem.

Or maybe your girlfriend is an outdoors-y kind of woman. She loves camping, hiking, and spending all her excess cash at REI, but your idea of camping means staying at a motel instead of a hotel. Two different passions, two different directions, one potentially huge problem to deal with as things get serious.

See, if the person you are dating seems to be going in a different direction than you in any regard, time can pass in the beginning when you are able to ignore it, but as the differences become more obvious or glaring, eventually the tension begins to dramatically increase. And the farther apart you are when the breakup happens, the more painful it will be because you've been together longer...just like a rubber band stretched to its breaking point. The farther your hands are apart when the snap happens, the more that rubber band will sting your skin when it breaks.

When he was a college student, a friend of mine named Ben was dating a girl for over a year. When nearly everyone he was close with questioned his developing relationship with this girl, he brushed them off. "You both seem to want very different things out of life," I told him one afternoon as we met over coffee on campus. Ben wanted to go into full-time missions when he graduated from college, and his girlfriend had no desire whatsoever to live a missionary lifestyle. She was raised with affluence, and living life on a missionary budget was something she had no intention of doing.

Ben gave many reasons for why he and his girlfriend should stay together, so I didn't push it too much. Eventually, they got more serious, and he bought a ring. And even with the warnings of many people in Ben's life (myself included) they got engaged. The wedding plans went into full swing, and Ben quickly realized that his new fiancé had pretty high expectations for what they would spend on their wedding.

Conflicts and financial arguments were a normal part of their weekly interactions, and Ben came to the realization that he didn't want to marry this girl. They broke off their engagement, and life just plain sucked for Ben and his ex. It took him a long time before he was able to connect with other people and activities again. Ben let the rubber band stretch too far for too long...and when it snapped, the pain was awful.

Are we going in the same direction? is an extremely important question to ask. When you are dating someone, this is one of the first things you want to consider. You'll avoid future pain if you're honest enough to address the potential relationship-ending issues now rather than later.

Of course, this is especially important in the spiritual aspect of your relationship. I have known and talked with many guys and girls who have compromised and have decided to settle for someone who just wasn't on the same level as they were in their walk with God, and time and time again, it has been a recipe for a relationship disaster. Sadly, Christian men and women are often guilty of compromise in this area, and when they do end up settling for someone they shouldn't settle for, they typically do it in different ways.

For example, guys frequently compromise and settle for someone when they start to become attracted to a girl physically. A friend of mine named Tom was attracted to a girl he knew in college. He was a follower of Christ, and she wasn't. They weren't at all spiritually aligned, so when they began dating, there were already quite a few points against them. Like many other stories I've told and you've probably heard, he ignored the advice of godly people around him in favor of "following his heart." They eventually got married, and sadly, two years after their wedding ceremony, his wife had an affair with a coworker and Tom's marriage ended.

Men are visually stimulated folk, and a girl's beauty can be the rationale for some bad decision making on the part of dudes who later discover that the girl has absolutely no relationship with God or any desire to walk closely with Him. I can't stress enough how important it is for men to make the priority of their heart Jesus, instead of a pretty face...even as hypnotizing as pretty faces can sometimes be.

So, we've seen the sorts of ways that men can compromise. Women, too, have their own tendencies and might settle for the wrong guy when they become emotionally drawn to a man who gives them the attention they desire. Ladies conventionally long for authentic connection, and a man who listens and cares can often win a woman's heart. I can name countless examples of Christian girls I know who have dated guys who claim to love them but have no desire to love Jesus.

Allison was a friend of mine from college who started dating a guy she knew from one of her classes. She was a follower of Christ, and her new boyfriend, Jason, wasn't. At the beginning of our freshman year, Allison was very much involved in our student Christian ministry on campus, but at Jason's promptings, she began attending less and less. Eventually, Allison stopped coming altogether, and I didn't see her much after that year. I knew Jason a little because we had some mutual friends in my dorm, and the truth is that he was a really nice guy. We sporadically hung out, and I liked him. He wasn't some evil guy who tried to lure Allison away from Jesus like a kidnapper with candy on a playground.

But from what he shared with me and a few other guys in my hall, I knew that Jason and Allison were sexually active by the time the spring semester rolled around, and knowing this made me sad.

The Allison I knew from the beginning of the year communicated her passion for Christ and sincerely followed His call to purity in her life at that time. And as you might guess, Allison's relationship with Jason didn't last either. Jason and Allison broke up the summer after our freshman year, and unfortunately, I didn't see her much more in our remaining time at college.

Regardless of the situation, when a Christian compromises, and settles for someone who doesn't have a passion for Jesus Christ, tough spiritual times lay ahead. The rubber band is going in opposite directions. And going in opposite directions (especially when it comes to your relationship with God) can be very harmful/hurtful to both parties involved if it's not addressed early on. I'm not saying that the course can't be corrected, but a Christian who desires a healthy, fruitful relationship with God has no business dating someone who doesn't care about following Christ wholeheartedly.

ARE YOU BOTH AUTHENTIC CHRISTIANS?

As you've seen in some of the examples I've shared, some followers of Christ are willing to compromise and date people who are't Christians. Nearly everything that I've mentioned in the previous section also applies here, but I want to go a little deeper because dating a non-believer can prove to be even more detrimental.

First, is there actually anything in the Bible that talks about connecting romantically with someone who doesn't follow Christ? In a word, no, there isn't anything specific that refers to dating a non-Christian, but we can most assuredly pull important principles from scripture about the business of doing life with those who don't know Jesus.

There is tremendous wisdom in 2 Corinthians 6:14:

Do not be yoked together with unbelievers. For what do righteousness and wickedness have in common? Or what fellowship can light have with darkness?

When read in context, this verse is actually making some intentional contrasts between believers and non-believers for the purpose of illustrating the subjects of idolatry, holiness, and premeditated connection with another person. Since it isn't directly addressing romantic relationships, it might be easy to dismiss this piece of Scripture and ignore the principles it intends to teach. This would be a mistake. When you sit down and contemplate the nature of what a marriage relationship is and the fact that it's a life-long covenant commitment that can essentially become the main focus of your world, there are quite a few similarities to passages that address idolatry, holiness, and an intimate connection with another person! If the precursor to marriage is dating, it shouldn't take much thought to connect the dots and realize that 2 Corinthians 6:14 is very applicable to any Christian's dating life.

What, exactly, is the verse saying? The verse refers specifically to this thing called a yoke. A yoke is a wooden crosspiece that is fastened over the necks of two animals (in biblical times, those animals were typically oxen) and attached to a plow or cart that they are to pull. In farming terms, if one ox was stronger or larger than the other, the plow would till the ground improperly because the strength of the two animals would be off-kilter and take the cart/plow in a skewed direction. It was of great importance that both oxen be equally yoked so that the farmer could maximize his work. Do you see the connection here to relationships and dating?

If Jesus is number one in your life, why would you want to "fasten" or "yoke" yourself to someone who doesn't understand this? And as I've just said, you marry someone whom you've dated, so why would you want to date someone who has nothing in common with you spiritually? If you are unequally yoked in your dating relationship, the cart of your life will be off-kilter and take you in hurtful, skewed directions that lead to heartbreak.

The idea here is to have enough patience not to settle for someone who doesn't know Jesus, have a relationship with Him, or claim His lordship in his or her life. Yes, I know—pretty girls can be really nice...and pretty. But if that good-looking face doesn't encourage you to walk closer with Jesus or challenge you to be a Spirit-filled man of God when life becomes difficult, you've yoked yourself unequally.

And yes, I know—sensitive men who listen to you when you talk and lavish you with the affection you crave and deserve can be so wonderfully refreshing...especially if they're cute. But if that cute, attentive-to-your-needs guy doesn't lead you spiritually or point you more toward your First Love, you've fastened yourself to someone who's just not good enough for you. Plain and simple.

I have heard far too many stories of young Christian men and women who settle and yoke themselves unequally to others who don't follow Christ, and the outcome is generally one of two scenarios. 1) They either end up continually frustrated with their partners who don't ever seem to "come around" and decide to engage in a relationship with God, or 2) they end up walking away from their faith because their partners have dragged them down. In my opinion, both of these outcomes are unacceptable, so why even start down that path in the first place by choosing to date a non-Christian?

Now, let's explore one more important question we should ask ourselves as we look to develop a foundation of godliness in a dating relationship.

ARE THERE GODLY PEOPLE AROUND YOU?

Earlier in chapter two, I mentioned the importance of involving other people whom you trust in your dating relationship when it comes to physical boundaries and accountability in the area of sexual purity. Like I said, a couple should never date in isolation. But involving others in accountability for purity should only be the beginning of keeping your relationship in the light.

The Christian life is always meant to be experienced in the context of community and fellowship with other believers. When we begin to separate ourselves or break away from the pack, so to speak, a number of bad consequences start to creep into our lives. Those three enemies: the world, the sinful nature or "flesh," and the Devil, can easily gain a foothold and influence our decision making in a negative way. However, if we proactively involve other caring believers in our lives, they are often able to spot areas in which we might be prone to compromise and succumb to temptation.

For dating couples, the urge to isolate frequently rises up and it can be tempting to cut other people out. "My dating life is nobody else's business," someone might say, or "We just want to be left alone because we don't get enough time with just the two of us."

As true as both of these statements might be (depending on your specific dating relationship), it's never a good idea to pursue seclusion when you're dating someone. Removing other important friends or family members from your romantic endeavors propagates compromise in sexual purity (as we've already discussed), a lack of accountability, an unhealthy obsession with the person you're dating, a waning interest in the world beyond your boyfriend/girlfriend, a diminishing healthy communication with others, and a ton of other bad stuff.

We've all seen it before, I'm sure. Guy gets girlfriend, guy disappears to hang out with only his girlfriend, friends of guy get mad because guy disappeared, guy gets dumped, guy wonders where all his friends are to help him through his rough time after the breakup, friends say, "You were the one that left, not us."

Or maybe you haven't seen something like that before, but you at least know what I'm talking about, right? I can personally think of a few examples of couples who date and spend every waking moment together, only to leave in the dust the friends who loved them. The relationships ended between the couples, and it was like they had to go crawling back to their friends to ask forgiveness for their abandonment. If saying yes to a dating relationship means saying no to your friends and family, you should probably reconsider the type of dating relationship you're currently in.

I would have felt horrible if my wife had stopped regularly engaging with her friends because she was dating me. When we were dating, in no way did I want to rob her of those precious friendships she enjoyed just because I was her boyfriend. Sure, we wanted to spend a lot of time together when we were dating, but like any other thing in our lives, we needed healthy boundaries. Besides, I always told her that one of the things I liked about her the most was the loyalty she had to her friends. If I changed all that when I entered the scene, I would be changing who she was as a person, and that would've been tragic.

You need godly people in your life to give you balance and perspective. You need input from friends and family who are wiser than you. You need to be willing to set an example for young believers around you who crave guidance on how a godly relationship should be done. You need people in your life! And if you want your relationship to include healthiness on every level, you cannot date in a vacuum devoid of others.

I'm not saying that in your dating relationship it becomes everyone else's business to the point that too many people are giving you unsolicited advice on every tiny detail of your life. That would be extreme, to say the least. I'm saying that you should involve the people you trust the most. People who know you and make godly contributions to your life. People like your parents, your best friend, the person who disciples you, your roommate, your pastor, and your siblings. The kind of folks who will ask you the tough questions about maintaining physical boundaries and the spiritual health of your relationship.

Men should be asked if they are leading their girlfriends toward Jesus and serving them sacrificially. Women should be asked if they are pointing their boyfriends toward Christ and encouraging them to be in love with their Savior. Without these kinds of questions, motivations start to slip, guards come down, and the hypnotizing lure of sin can quickly creep in and ruin a godly dating relationship.

A couple in isolation is a couple in danger, so surround yourselves with godly men and women who care about you and care about Jesus. If you do, you'll be laying the right kind of building blocks that shape a foundation, bringing honor to the Lord.

ILL COMMUNICATION

Because I've worked with college students for the majority of my adult life, I've spent a significant amount of time doing a lot of immature, non-adult things. All-night movie marathons, weekly poker games with ten other dudes in a non-heated lawnmower shed during the dead of winter, furniture-clearing dance parties throughout an entire house with 500 random strangers, prank wars involving raw fish under a sink and coffee grounds neatly packed within the victim's shower head spigot, party games that regularly incorporate pantyhose on my head, and countless get-to-know-you questions in order to break the ice at the beginning of group events or weekend retreats.

I've been asked many personal questions during my many moments on the "hot seat" at college student get-togethers, and there isn't a whole lot that can rattle me when the questions are fired in my direction. One of the benefits of being part of so many events at which information is swapped freely is that I've given a lot of answers to common questions young people like to ask.

When my relationship status moved from "single" to "married," I began to give a lot of thought to the thing or things I like the most about being married and what I believed to be the most important element of a healthy marriage relationship. When someone would ask me what this element was, the routine Christian answer I usually gave involved a significant amount of commentary about finding a mate who loved Jesus. Inevitably, I would be sure to mention another trait I felt was of extreme importance.

"What?" students would ask, because every breathing college student wants to know what a married person believes is most important in a relationship. And I would never hesitate to tell them.

"Communication," I would answer. And I still believe I'm right.

CRYSTAL CLEAR

If you know anything about the military or you happen to be familiar with the process that the military goes through when it's time to get a job done, you know about the profound importance that is placed on clear communication and military personnel following through with any given orders. This is especially true in times of war. The communication that happens must be deliberate and precise if the mission is to be accomplished with the least amount of collateral damage.

I like the way this point is made near the end of the movie

A Few Good Men,[7] when the hotshot lawyer Lt. Daniel Kaffee (played by Tom Cruise) puts the intimidating Col. Nathan Jessup (played by Jack Nicholson) on the witness stand in order to bring clarity to a case involving the untimely death of a young private at a marine base.

There's a series of intentional questions that Kaffee asks Jessup just to tick him off, and the very power-hungry/snarky Col. Jessup fires back a few questions of his own toward the lawyer to try to prove the point that his orders are law. There are consequences to disobeying his law, and the communication that comes from on high should always be taken seriously. Here's a quick snippet of the dialogue during the drama-filled courtroom scene:

Jessup: *You ever served in an infantry unit, son?*

Kaffee: *No, sir.*

Jessup: *Ever served in a forward area?*

Kaffee: *No, sir.*

Jessup: *Ever put your life in another man's hands...asked him to put his life in yours?*

Kaffee: *No, sir.*

Jessup: *We follow orders, son. We follow orders or people die. It's that simple. Are we clear?*

Kaffee: *Yes, sir.*

Jessup: *ARE WE CLEAR?!*

Kaffee: *Crystal.*

When it comes to understanding the importance of clarity in communication, the stakes are high in life or death situations. We follow orders or people die...it's that simple.

Now, I'd be willing to bet that most of you aren't ever going to be in a situation involving a scenario that determines whether you live or die because of communication, but I think the military example with Lt. Kaffee and Col. Jessup underscores the point nicely. Orders are to be clear and understood fully so that lives won't be put in danger. Communication is of the utmost importance in nearly anything involving a plan, a goal, a desire, and certainly a relationship.

COMMUNICATION 101

I was a communications minor back in college. "Whoop-dee-doo," you might say, "a communications *minor*?" Yes, I know that means absolutely nothing when I'm trying to highlight the idea that I'm somewhat qualified to wade into the deep-end of the interactions people have with one another, but at the very least I can tell you that I took a few classes at the university level involving research into the more complex levels of communication.

To this day, I distinctly remember sitting in a lecture hall of about 400 students and listening to my professor discuss methods for talking to us in ways we could understand. My brain starts to hurt a little bit when I think about what that last sentence actually means, but you're probably smarter than I am, so my guess is that you know what my professor meant.

It's essentially Communication 101, and the breakdown is fairly straightforward from beginning-to-end regarding what needs to happen on the journey of a certain subject. Let's start with thinking of a topic I might theoretically want someone to clearly understand in the way *I'm* able to understand it. For the sake of illustration, I'm going to choose the topic of Captain America's abdominal muscles.

If I want you to know everything I know about Captain America's abs, and I want to make sure that you understand the Captain's abs the way I understand them, it's important that I'm keenly aware of what will happen when I start to talk with you about this very important issue.

Every topic, issue, idea, or argument starts out in its purest form as the deliverer's interpretation of that subject. I believe that Captain America's abs are ripped, and I think you should know that truth, too. Therefore, my topic must then pass through what the communication world calls my "grid." My grid is my personal way of understanding, reasoning or problem solving. It incorporates my communication style and takes into account my personality; it is affected by my history and the way I was raised; it involves my social awareness and how I am able to interact with others. Basically, my grid is my way of communicating.

So, after my topic passes through my grid, we come to the point when I actually communicate it to you:

Oh, man! Do you know how awesome Captain America's abs are? They are so ripped! See, Steve Rogers was a frail and sickly young man who wanted to serve his country, so he volunteered for a top-secret performance-enhancing experiment during which he was taken to a laboratory in Washington, D.C. and injected with a Super-Soldier Serum. After the doctors administered the secret serum, Steve Rogers emerged from this special vita-ray chamber with a perfect human body. He was then put through a series of tests and training exercises that crafted him into who we now know as Captain America. He can do like, I don't know, a million sit-ups, and it shows because he has washboard abs that you can scrub your laundry on. They're amazing!

When it's communicated (albeit with a certain amount of bizarre enthusiasm), the topic must then pass through what is called "noise." Noise can be anything in the immediate environment that can dilute the purity of the message. This can be actual audible noise, a cell phone buzzing in your pocket, a bad attitude on your part, a child pulling on your clothes, or a bear wrestling a chimpanzee in the background behind my shoulder as I speak to you. Anything that distracts or "waters down" the message being communicated is referred to as "noise."

The message then takes an obvious course of action during which it is received by you. It passes through your grid (which is totally different than mine) and then becomes your interpretation of the communicated idea. The goal in all of this, of course, is that my idea of the subject be exactly the same as your idea of the subject.

Now, all of this may seem somewhat simple, but the reality is that we are all constantly misunderstood in life. For example, something I might be trying to tell someone might not come out of my mouth just right. Or the person I am talking to might be tired and distracted. Or the way this person processes information might not be the same as the way I process information, so we get the sense that the entire conversation is one big miss. Stuff like that. You know what I'm talking about, don't you?

Communication, in theory, is easy. Communication, in reality, is hard. My point in all of this is to help you understand how complex communication really can be. It's a lot more than just "talking with someone." When people attempt to share information with one another and they try to make their ideas on a subject exactly the same as someone else's ideas on that subject, a lot can get in the way to interrupt the flow. And because someone might have a frustrating history with some various past miscommunications, the temptation in the present is to communicate as little as possible as to not relive the discomfort of the past. Believe me, I understand that mindset, but communicating less with someone is, was, and always will be a bad idea. Especially with someone you're dating.

A BAD EXAMPLE

When there is a distinct lack of communication in any dating relationship, a few things inevitably rise to the surface that will ultimately lead to the end of the relationship. I personally have experienced some of those repercussions due to little-to-no communication when I was dating a girl, and I must say that the repercussions aren't healthy or life-giving.

Sure, it's easy to act cool like nothing is wrong when someone asks how the girlfriend or boyfriend is doing, but that ache in the pit of your stomach tells a different story, doesn't it? If communication dwindles, fear and anxiety begin to grow. Without a steady stream of dialogue between two people who are dating, the pair often begin to wonder what exactly is happening in the relationship. And man-oh-man was this true of the relationship I had with the girl I was dating my senior year of college.

About halfway through my senior year at Virginia Tech, a young girl named Sara caught my attention and drew me in like a tractor beam. She was fun-loving, pretty, and she loved Jesus...the trifecta. I asked her out on a date, and very quickly afterward, we put the official "dating" label on our relationship. All was well for quite a few months, and I was pretty sure we had a good thing going that would last beyond my impending graduation from school. Sara was an interesting girl, though. She would often be very communicative, friendly, and attentive to me as her boyfriend, but every now and then she would just shut down and stop talking to me altogether.

It was strange. Days would go by when she would be too busy to hang out with me, and when I would call to try to connect and see how she was, she'd either not answer or be very short with me on the phone like she was upset about something. I would inevitably ask if she was okay, and she'd respond with, "I'm fine."

And then, just like nothing had happened, the next day would come and she'd call me or drop by my apartment or meet me somewhere on campus and act like nothing had been wrong at all. I didn't want to rehash what might have been wrong with her, so I just accepted this friendly version of my girlfriend and didn't bring up the fact that she had been pretty distant. Simply put, we didn't talk about it.

Our relationship went on like this during my final months at college. Things would be great between us, she would have a distant spell for a few days, she'd snap out of it, and we'd go right back to being normal again. I liked her a lot, so I put up with it.

Looking back on this, however, I have the desire to travel back in time to meet up with my former self, smack my own face, and ask, "Do you like waking up every morning wondering whether or not she actually wants to date you today? Do you really want to be with someone who doesn't communicate with you for days at a time about what's going on with her life? Is that the kind of woman you want to marry?"

I can't time travel to ask myself those questions, but I wish I could. The relationship story ends, of course, with her being very distant during the summer months we were apart after I graduated from college, and the obvious break up that should have happened long before it actually did. To this day, I still don't know what bothered her so much that she refused to engage with me during those distant spells, but I wish I would't have settled for it the way I did when it was happening.

The consistent lack of communication between the two of us made me very insecure about our relationship, my ability to be a good boyfriend, and my appeal as a person. Bad relationships have a tendency to do that, don't they? They can really derail us because they permeate into every available space in our minds and hearts. If Sara would have told me what was going on with her in those times, I would have been able to do a number of things differently that may have led to a far better outcome.

I could have given her more space instead of continually trying to reach out to her when she needed her own time. I could have pro-actively prayed for her if she was struggling with something difficult. I could have evaluated whether or not this relationship was something I wanted in my life far earlier than I did. But she never talked with me about her distant spells, so I was left to wonder...which lead to distance and my unhealthy scrutiny.

Communication is essential and vital to the health of any dating relationship because without a steady stream of verbal connection between a couple, both are left wondering about a variety of potentially negative things that draw the focus away from a life of walking closely with Jesus.

LET'S GET PHYSICAL

Another bad repercussion that pops up when communication dies down is a shift in the primary focus of what the relationship is about. If a couple is communicating well and regularly, they are able to grow close to one another in a healthy and godly way that, as I heard a football coach once say, "keeps the main thing the main thing."

If they neglect to engage in ample amounts of conversation, however, sinful defaults have a tendency to kick in, and the main thing becomes a physical thing. You know exactly what I'm referring to here...

"Welp, we're not talking about anything...and she seems to be as bored as I am...so why don't we just make out for the next two hours?"

And once you start down that road, it's extremely difficult to course-correct. The relationship begins to revolve solely around the physical, and you never truly get to know the other person because you're never truly communicating with that person. You end up training your mind and body to think and react to your dating partner in a certain way that equals an extended time of foreplay. It almost becomes a Pavlovian response, so to a knee-jerk reaction to being with that person. "Time with my boyfriend means make out time," or "being with my girlfriend means fooling around time."

But continual acts of foreplay, instead of healthy times of communication, are the antithesis of a good relationship. Foreplay is like a freeway on-ramp. Its purpose is to transition you to full speed. You don't see cars hanging out on on-ramps, never intending to get on the freeway, but many dating couples build their relationships this way. Song of Solomon 2:7 says,

Do not arouse or awaken love until it so desires.

This is great advice (surprise, surprise) that helps each of us to understand that it is foolish to dive into the physical aspect of a relationship instead of communicating with a dating partner. Communication will build a thriving friendship, and a good friendship will set you up for a strong marriage far more than a physical connection ever will.

GAMES

I've talked a bit about how a lack of communication can lead to constant wondering about the status of the relationship and how it can shift a relationship toward a solely physical existence that isn't honoring to God. However, there is another inappropriate and strangely popular side effect to little-to-no communication—the manipulative tactic called "playing relationship games."

When I say *games*, of course, I'm not referring to busting out *Settlers of Catan* on a Saturday night and enjoying some healthy competition. What I'm talking about here is the specific scheming that can go on between two people who are dating one another in an attempt to elicit a certain response from their partner. Essentially, it's intentional manipulation for the purposes of either getting something you want, subtly asserting your dominance, or triggering that unexplained jolt of adrenaline one gets when tampering with someone's emotions and his or her heart is on the line.

Games are carefully crafted manifestations of selfishness, and they do nothing but hurt other people. You can see examples of relationship games all the time in romantic comedies, dramatic television, or your run-of-the-mill elementary school playground. For the sake of clarity, let's outline a typical playground case of "relationship manipulation."

A little boy playing on the monkey bars likes a little girl who's playing on the swings, so he walks up to her, pushes her off of her swing, punches her in the arm, and as she screams for the teacher, he pulls her hair. Now, why would this little boy do this to a little girl whom he supposedly likes? Because pushing her off the swing, punching her in the arm, and pulling her hair "means something." The little boy will then get punished by the teacher and subsequently teased by every other little boy on the playground afterward as they chant, "YOU'VE GOT A GIRLFRIEND! YOU'VE GOT A GIRL-FRIEND!" over and over again. The little boy doesn't mind, though, because these are the necessary consequences one must be willing to put up with for the sake of love.

Ridiculous? Of course it is. When we see relationship games played out in such an absurd display, we scoff at the methods the little boy uses to prove his love to the little girl by doing one thing, yet meaning something totally different. Truthfully, however, many other "grown up" relationship games are peppered throughout our lives all the time. Girls say one thing, but they mean another. Guys will act a certain way one evening, but then act another way the next day. She will send a cryptic text to see how he will respond. He will act interested in another girl just to make her jealous. Juvenile stuff.

I've seen guys manipulate women by hanging out with a girl's best friend and drop hints about how he's single just to see if the girl's friend will mention anything about the girl. I've seen girls intentionally leave a social media status up in hopes that the guy they like will take the bait and get in touch with them about what they've posted. Nothing seems to be off limits when it comes to manipulating someone in order to get what you want. Even one of the most popular secular relationship books in publication, entitled *The Rules*[8], is basically a step-by-step guide on how to manipulate a man into pursuing you by playing games. Sure, we see the example of the little boy on the playground and label it as nonsensical, but the truth is we are buying into the exact same relationship philosophy if we are playing games with one another instead of communicating with openness and honesty.

I came across this verse in my early years as a follower of Jesus Christ, and it stirred something inside me as I pondered the challenge it gave to my life:

> When I was a child, I spoke like a child, I thought like a child, I reasoned like a child. When I became a man, I gave up childish ways. (1 Corinthians 13:11)

Little boys and little girls send mixed messages that are supposed to "mean something." But when little boys and little girls become men and women, they give up childish ways and communicate with one another. Healthy communication is the antidote to the poison of manipulation and games. When we are clear about our intentions and uninterested in messing around with another person's heart, roads are opened toward vulnerability, trust, honesty, and eventually a strong bond.

The temptation in dating and relationships is to go for the quick thrill of deceit or game-playing, but our hearts are precious treasures that deserve better treatment. When I was single, I was on the lookout for someone I could trust, but when you know that you are being manipulated, that trust is broken. Like me, my guess is that you are probably unwilling to lay your heart on the line when the relationship feels risky because someone might be playing games. Each of us deserve better in a relationship, so don't settle for someone who is prone to childish ways.

"Quit playing games with my heart," sing the Backstreet Boys from the late 1990s. I agree.

LISTEN UP

The book of Proverbs is simply incredible. There is so much wisdom packed into only thirty-one chapters, and yet the book itself often speaks to how one could be a wiser person.

With all of its wisdom, it speaks specifically about the importance of listening. Proverbs 18:13 says,

To answer before listening—that is folly and shame.

I like this, but I have to be honest and say that I like the para-phrased version of the verse in *The Message* a bit better: "Answering before listening is both stupid and rude."[9] Oh, snap.

Listening is such an important part of the communication process, yet it's often the most neglected. From a very young age, we are trained to speak *at* people instead of *with* people because we place a high value on being heard. Interestingly, we have a very difficult time absorbing what another person is saying to us because we're constantly thinking about what we're going to say next when someone is speaking.

Social media and technology have reinforced this way of thinking via text messages that communicate *at* someone, online posts that talk *at* someone, profile statuses that pronounce our feelings *at* someone. We think we're communicating in a healthy way because we've never been more "connected," but the truth is if everyone is talking, no one is listening. And if nobody is listening, all that "communication" we think we're participating in has turned into noise. If half of the equation is missing, all of the equation is missing. This is an especially important point to be aware of when it comes to communication in the realm of dating.

If you aren't listening, you aren't communicating. If you aren't communicating, you aren't connecting. And if you aren't connecting, you are on your way to isolation...meaning you're on your way to a breakup.

Listening well communicates care, affection, and love. It silently tells the other person that what he or she has to say is valuable enough to garner careful contemplation. I always feel more loved when my wife listens to me because it makes me feel understood and known. Truthfully, if I feel listened to when I'm communicating something to my wife, she could completely disagree with everything I've said and I would still feel like it was a productive conversation. Why? Because she has made an extended effort to move toward me by proactively listening to my opinion, and that communicates love.

We all want to make sure we're heard when we talk with someone (especially if the talk leans toward argument), but probably the best way to do this is to work on our listening skills. Instead of always succumbing to the desire to speak, I think many people would be better off in their relationships if they proactively listened. A helpful acronym that someone once shared with me is applicable here: W.A.I.T. When you are engaged in a conversation with another person, ask yourself the question, "Why Am I Talking?" When you think it over, it's a pretty good question that can help shape you into a better listener, making you an all-around more desirable person to spend time with. Having the label of "good listener" is always a positive character trait when you're dating someone. Everybody loves a good listener, so it's high time we pursue this quality attribute with zeal.

One of my best friends, Brett, is an exceptional listener. This is one of my favorite qualities about him, and it gives him such a warm personality. Brett will listen not only to his friends and family, but often to random strangers.

I remember going out to dinner with a bunch of friends one night, including Brett, and after giving the waitress our orders, we each closed our menus and continued talking with each other. However, when it came time for Brett to place his order, he asked the waitress what her name was. He asked where she went to school, found out she was a ceramics enthusiast, and then he even talked with her about how his favorite description of God in the Bible was that He is the Potter. Brett knew more about this girl after placing his order for dinner than most people might find out about another person on a first date. And why? Because he asked her good questions, and he listened to her when she spoke.

I love that so much about my friend, Brett. It comes so naturally to him, but I need to work hard at being a good listener. The old adage of "practice makes perfect" applies well here.

So, in the name of becoming better listeners, let me share a few helpful tips I've picked up over the years as I've studied people, including the various communication tactics effective listeners use. Hopefully, a careful study of this subject will vastly improve the quality of your dating relationship.

1. Ask smart questions when someone is finished communicating so he or she has the opportunity to further clarify what was said. Don't you love it when someone asks you a great question? You get the sense that this person genuinely cares about you and

your insight into the topic at hand. Asking good questions communicates interest, and interest is an important thing to express when you're dating someone. Be careful, however, not to ask too many questions or inappropriately timed questions when someone is speaking. Continually interrupting someone's train of thought with various questions can be more annoying than endearing. Listen well and ask well.

2. When someone is talking, reflectively listen to what he or she is trying to convey. When a person reflectively listens, he or she repeats back what was heard in a way that shows he or she was paying attention to what was being said. You have to be careful here too, though, because reflective listening is a skill that requires a bit of delicacy and balance. If it's done wrong, it can come off as irritating or condescending. You don't want to repeat everything you hear back to the communicator, just important main points that tell the other person you are following his or her thoughts and tracking what he or she is trying to get across. This establishes clarity between two people.

3. Affirm what someone is saying and resist the temptation to attack when you disagree with his or her opinion. It's easy to find flaws in people's thinking or reasoning, especially when the topic of discussion is something you are passionate about. But verbally jumping all over someone won't be productive and will most likely deeply hurt the one you're conversing with. Affirmation doesn't necessarily mean you have to agree completely with what the person is saying, but there are always touch points within a dialogue on which you can find common ground. Affirming those areas of agreement instead of attacking the person on points of

disagreement can smooth out some topic tension and lower the guard of the one who's speaking to you. When you affirm just a few things that someone says, he or she feels listened to and appreciated. This person will be more likely to respond to you with warmth instead of coldness.

These three areas are a great place to start if you desire to be a better listener. However, I must pause here and remind you that even though I'm dishing out advice on how to listen well, I am not claiming to be an expert. Sometimes I surprise myself at how bad I am at listening, especially when certain things like anger get thrown into the mix. For some reason, when I get mad, my eardrums close and a healthy portion of my sensibility withers away. I'm disappointed at my listening skills when I'm angry, but I continue to pray that the Lord will grant me the maturity to become a better listener as I walk closer with Him. I know my wife would be pleased if that were to happen James 1:19 says:

My dear brothers and sisters, take note of this: Everyone should be quick to listen, slow to speak and slow to become angry.

You know it's time to whip out a pen and underline something in the Bible when it blatantly states "take note of this." Being a person who is quick to listen, slow to speak, and slow to anger is like being a person who is beautiful, athletic, kind, humble, and able to juggle chainsaws to raise money for children's charity. In other words, they're rare.

I love it, though, because God's word sets the bar high for our lives. It would be a huge bummer if the Bible stated something like,

"Listen to people when you aren't distracted, keep the cussing to a minimum, and don't hit someone more than twice if they hit you first." The Lord wants us to live our lives with excellence, and even though it may seem impossible at times, He gives us the power to do it through the Holy Spirit.

When we allow the Holy Spirit to work in and through us on a moment-by-moment basis, we are tapping into the ultimate power source for a life completely glorifying to God and completely exhilarating for us to live. He is the One who makes it possible for us to listen well, communicate with clarity and maturity, honor our bodies by resisting sexual temptation, and focus appropriately on others so they can understand what we are trying to say. Yielding our lives to the Holy Spirit's influence will make our relationships the best they can possibly be because when He is in control, we become better communicators and James 1:19 becomes not just a possibility, but a reality.

LET ME SUM UP

A good and godly communicator is someone who cares deeply about the one he or she is dating. He or she understands the value of open and honest communication and is intentional about going the extra mile to bring clarity to certain subjects that might be confusing or difficult to wade through. This person will not self-focus in the midst of interaction with the other person, but he or she will be purposeful in being "others centered" via active listening to communicate care and affection. This person gives others the gift of listening.

A good and godly communicator doesn't play emotional games with the heart of a boyfriend or girlfriend. He or she is careful and discerning about what to say, how much to say, and the specific timing for saying something to lovingly protect the other.

Sadly, there aren't many worthwhile examples of men and women who have gone before us to show this generation how it should be done, and the norm has become the polar opposite of wholesome communication. But God calls each of His followers to something much greater than the hollow models the world has pushed forth, and the ability to be great communicators is achieved when we walk closely with Him and rely on His power to shape our character.

Good communication is of paramount importance in a dating relationship. In my opinion, it may be the most important aspect. Valuing communication when you're single sets the stage nicely for the future, and allowing the Lord to make you a better communicator is certainly one of the most attractive things you can offer to someone when your relationship status changes.

YOU GOT SERVED

Back in my single years, I worked in full-time Christian ministry at James Madison University in Harrisonburg, Virginia. I loved working directly with the college students there on campus, primarily because of the caliber of student men who were involved. Simply put, they were quality dudes.

One of the things that impressed me about the guys in our ministry at JMU was their desire to reach out to the rest of the student body and serve them. A great example of this is when the guys went on custodial duty. Someone had the idea to divide the guys in our ministry into pairs and send them out to knock on dorm room doors and offer to clean toilets.

Yes, our men were traveling around the on-campus living facil-
ities, armed with toilet brushes, cleaner, and happy attitudes. They
would say they were with the student ministry and wanted to offer
their services by cleaning the toilet. If the resident said "yes," the
guys would quickly enter the bathroom, scrub the commode until it
was sparkling, and then move on to the next room. They didn't pass
out any pamphlets; they didn't share any specific message with the
residents in that moment; they just enjoyed serving people with no
strings attached.

This impressed me for a variety of reasons. First, toilets in general
are disgusting, but toilets that are used solely by men are disgusting on
an absurd level, so offering to repeatedly clean male-used toilet after
male-used toilet is crazy to me. Second, our guys didn't do just one
dorm and then move on...they visited every men's dorm on campus,
and at the time, there were around 15,000 students going to JMU.
I don't know exactly how many were living in the men's dorms, but
my assumption is—a lot. Third, this kind of service reminded me a lot
of the foot washing Jesus did with His disciples. It was a way for our
men to communicate to the other students that they believed it was
important for Christians to serve others, period. No strings attached.
They were there to do the dirty work, and they did it with a smile.

I love telling this story because it encourages me to have a better
attitude toward intentional service and humility, even when I don't
feel like it. Additionally, today it's impossible for anyone to go door-
to-door in a university dormitory because of increased security, so it
forces me to think more creatively about how we can serve people in
the name of the gospel.

"THEY ARE SO HOT…I JUST HAVE TO SERVE THEM?"

I'd be willing to bet that dating's major selling point is not the glitz and glamour of "serving another person." In fact, I would be really surprised if that were one of the top ten reasons for anyone to enter into a dating relationship. One doesn't intrinsically think, "It would be really great to date that girl so I can serve her sacrificially." We simply aren't wired that way because the undercurrent in every human heart is selfishness. Our sinful nature makes it nearly impossible to push service to the front of the line when it comes to our main motivation for dating.

We view dating through the lens of "what can this relationship do for me?" Of course, we don't *actually* ask ourselves that question when we're single and ready to mingle (oh, man…did I just use that phrase?), but the truth is, it's probably the main reason everyone jumps into the dating pool head-first.

Think about it. When you look back on your motivations for getting into a relationship in the past, what were they? If you're having trouble, let me help you along with a few of mine from the past:

- Man, she is so hot. I would love to date her.
- I would feel so much better about myself if I had a girl in my life to tell me she loves me.
- People would respect me more if I could get a girl like her to date me…they would think that I'm awesome.

I could go on with other horrifying revelations from my past about why I chose to date the girls I did, but I won't. Now, reading these, you might have judged me for my deep-seeded selfishness, but the truth is, these *were* my major motivations when I was single and sharkin' for the ladies. And if we're honest, we all know these motivations are universal. When it comes down to it, the underlying motivator for dating is that it's "all about me."

What will that person do for me? How will he or she make me feel? What will he or she do to serve me? Improve my reputation? Satisfy me and my cravings? Me. Me. Me. When it comes to dating, we are takers.

But this shouldn't be so. Dating should not be about taking and focusing on what another person can do for me...it should be about how I can serve the one I am privileged enough to date.

TICKS AND DEMENTORS

When I was younger, I remember being terrified of blood-sucking ticks. So much so, that one time, when my grandparents were showing us a plot of land they were interested in buying, I would not get out of the car. The land was in an extremely wooded area, and I remember thinking that ticks were likely waiting to jump from the tree limbs onto my head so they could burrow into my scalp and suck my blood. I hated ticks more than any other creature, I think.

Now, this is the nature of a tick. Its whole purpose in life is to take. For example, a tick will attach itself to a deer or dog or some other animal and suck blood. It gives nothing back to the animal it is attached to, except maybe a disease. It simply latches on and takes.

Similarly, a Dementor, from the world of Harry Potter, has the same kind of motivation. The Harry Potter Wiki[10] (yes, there is such a thing) defines a *Dementor* as a creature that feeds off of human happiness and thus causes depression and despair to anyone near them. They can also consume a person's soul, leaving their victims in a permanent vegetative state. Dementors are often referred to as "soul-sucking fiends" and are known to leave a person as an empty-shell.

Both a Dementor and a tick are takers, and you can probably think of a few people in dating relationships who share similar qualities with the fictional Harry Potter character and the very real insect. They latch on to another person and take from them on every occasion possible. They look to fulfill their own needs and desires, yet give nothing back, leaving the other person as an empty-shell.

Alright, maybe I'm being a bit melodramatic, but I want and need to drive this point home. You never see a tick attaching itself to another tick, do you? A Dementor never attacks another Dementor and tries to suck out its soul. Why? Because two takers in a relationship makes no natural sense. The relationship *sucks*. (Sorry, I just couldn't help myself.) The reality in relationships, however, is that a lot of ticks are dating ticks, and a lot of Dementors are dating Dementors.

A DIFFERENT PERSPECTIVE

Of course, when it's all written out like this, my guess is that most any decent person would recoil at this notion of being a "blood-sucking life taker," but sadly, it is the cultural norm. We look to culture to tell us how to have a relationship, and we get beer commercials, tabloid postings, and reality TV that scream at us, "This is the right way to do it!" And most of the time, we buy it. We pick up a magazine at the grocery store checkout line and see the cover exclaim to us the way to get the most pleasure out of sex, so we purchase it. We religiously watch every episode of *The Bachelor* and see a man claim to be in love with the final woman contestant who made it to the end, when just yesterday he was making out in a hot tub with the other two finalists he didn't pick. Celebrity couples marry, and they get divorced...and this feels like the norm. We think that relationships are all about us and what the other person can do for us, but Jesus taught something radically different.

> *But whoever would be great among you must be your servant, and whoever would be first among you must be your slave, even as the Son of Man came not to be served but to serve, and to give his life as a ransom for many. (Matthew 20:26b-28)*

We are called not to be takers in a dating relationship, but givers. Givers are servants who see Christ Himself as a model instead of modern culture, which begs us to fulfill our own needs and desires. Jesus came not to be served but to serve, and this should be our primary goal as we look toward dating. Before sin entered the picture, humanity was designed to give, serve, and love. Jesus lived this out as the perfect example, and the cool thing is we can do that now...even in our modern American approach to dating.

When both people in a dating relationship are looking to give and pour into one another, they are a beautiful model of what a healthy relationship should be, and they set an incredible example for others to emulate. They also set themselves up well for the possibility of marriage because any married couple can tell you that being married is about serving the other person and dying to yourself, not selfishly taking. That's right—the primary reason for getting married is to give to the other person, not to get something for yourself.

I've seen a number of people live out this mindset of service within a dating relationship, and it has been extremely encouraging for me to witness what a godly couple looks like when serving the other person is the priority. Let me give you a few practical examples of what I mean:

1. I know a guy who would do a monthly "favorites" date with his girlfriend. He'd put the time and forethought into planning a series of things to do during a day or evening that were his girlfriend's favorite things. She loved the outdoors, so they would do things like go for a walk, go on a bike ride, enjoy a picnic outside, etc. She also loved ice cream, so he would intentionally plan to visit every local ice cream place in the area, checking them off one by one. Nothing too over-the-top or crazy, but their monthly favorites date communicated to her that she was special and her interests were his priority.

2. My wife's roommate back in college had a boyfriend who knew how much she loved Disney, so he planned a surprise trip to Orlando. He showed up at her place at 4:00 o'clock in the morning and flashed her the tickets he had to Disney World. They drove to the airport, flew to Florida, and spent the day together at the "most magical place on earth." I was floored when I heard about what he did (mostly because I was thinking about how much money it must have cost), but I was also super impressed with his desire to serve and care for his girlfriend in a fun, surprising way.

3. Okay, here's a personal one that I did for the woman who would become my bride. After my wife, Rachael, and I had been dating for only about three months, we were forced to

spend the summer apart because I was heading to Daytona Beach, Florida for a summer missions project, and she was flying to the other side of earth to study abroad in Florence, Italy. I wanted her to enjoy her trip and feel encouraged, so I created "Rachael's Travel Survival Kit" for the plane to Europe. I made puzzles for her to solve, I wrote up quizzes for her to take, I drew black and white pictures for her to color, and I included a bunch of encouraging Scripture verses for her to read through as she flew. Yes, it was cheesy, but she liked that sort of thing, and I certainly loved making it for her. In fact, even now as I recall making that survival kit, a smile comes to my face because I absolutely loved doing it for her. Cheeeeeeeese.

4. One of the guys in my Bible study had a girlfriend who would routinely surprise him throughout their relationship with small but fun little delightful moments that communicated, "I'm thinking about you and I care about you." She'd do things like leave notes for him in places he would later find them, including fake parking tickets on his car that read, "This isn't a parking fine, but you're certainly fine!" Ugh, I know, I know...but he really loved it. In the fall, she would buy him a t-shirt or jersey of his favorite football team, and place it in his room along with a note that communicated to him she couldn't wait to watch the game with him come Sunday afternoon (even though she hated football). She would also do things like sneak into his place and clean his room and bathroom. She'd do his laundry when he was really busy with school (not all the time, of course—she made it clear to him

that she wasn't his mother), and she would bake him dessert-type treats when he needed to pull an all-nighter before a big test the next day. She was the picture of someone who cared about serving the guy she dated...and I loved being in their wedding when they both graduated from college.

All of these examples require discipline and a certain mindset because our default is to think solely about ourselves. The repercussions of serving someone you care about, however, are quite delightful.

I heard a friend once say, "It took me ten years to figure out that the biggest problem in my marriage was me." This implies, of course, that if you become comfortable in your own selfishness, you're going to have some major problems. There's no better way to prepare for a great marriage of giving than to start practicing the art of giving when you date. Let's look to Jesus Christ, the ultimate servant, as the trailblazer on how we should do relationships and serve one another. This will not only bolster great dating relationships, but will also shine brightly in the darkness of cultural dating, drawing others to the redeeming power of Christ's love and sacrifice.

LET'S JUST BE FRIENDS

*Friendship is unnecessary, like philosophy, like art...
it has no survival value; rather it is one of those things that
give value to survival.*[11] —C.S. Lewis

I'm a military brat. Now, if you're unfamiliar with that term, it basically means that I grew up in a military family (specifically, the Air Force) and we moved to a new location every few years. Growing up with that kind of lifestyle as the norm was difficult, to say the least, but the experience of constantly moving, time and time again, shaped me into the person I am today, and for that, I am extremely grateful.

Because moving became routine after (on average) every two years or so, making new friends was a large part of the adaptation process. It was important to be able to have friends who I enjoyed being around in a place that was completely foreign to me. And although I understood this concept quite well, I was a natural introvert and fairly inflexible when it came to pioneering new life adventures. Consequently, the common parental adage of "go make some new friends" was a rather large obstacle for me.

We all know that kids can be quite cruel, and because I frequently wore the unpopular label of "new kid," I became all too familiar with the notion of uncaring fellow grade-schoolers. One particular memory that springs to the forefront of my mind occurred during the beginning of my sophomore year of high school.

My freshman year was spent in Stafford, Virginia, surrounded by familiarity because of the rare four-year stint my dad spent stationed at the Pentagon in Washington, D.C. New orders meant a new home, so we packed up and headed off to Montgomery, Alabama, where I found myself as one of only two new kids at a small private Christian school, populated by predominantly white rich kids who enjoyed torturing almost anyone who showed any sign of weakness.

Cut and zoom to the metaphorical target indelibly printed on my face.

One particular day, after two weeks of sitting with the other new guy during lunch, he was invited to join the popular dudes at their table, which left me literally by myself at the end of a long cafeteria table with nothing but my peanut butter and jelly sandwich. Now, ask any high school kid and he will tell you that there is no worse time to fly solo than at lunch time. I was horrified. In fact, even now as I write the recounting of this story, I can still feel the knot in my stomach that quickly formed when I found myself all alone in the cafeteria that day.

One of the nicer girls in the school eventually extended to me a merciful invitation to join her and her friends for the remainder of lunchtime, and I breathed a small sigh of relief as I joined them.

In that moment during my sophomore year in the cafeteria, all I wanted was a friend to sit with so I could feel accepted in a new school. And when I think about it, I still desire the kind of friendships I craved back then, but now I crave in a different way. Having real friends in your life is an important part of your well-being because (as we've talked about already, albeit in a different context) it is not good for people to be alone (Genesis 2:18).

IT IS BY DESIGN

Each and every person walking this planet needs to be connected in some way to another human being or beings. This is just a fact. And the piece of evidence that proves my point lies in the punishment prescribed to any individual who is deemed unworthy to interact with others. I'm talking about the penalty one must pay if he or she acts badly when already in a place of punishment—solitary confinement.

We've all seen the movies or television shows that reveal to us the worst of the worst and take us into the jail cells of people who have been really, really bad. So much so that they can't even be allowed to spend time with any of the other criminals. They are locked away all alone by themselves. As people, we understand that dishing out the sentence of solitary confinement is a pretty serious consequence because it strips a person of the necessary human contact each and every one of us crave. This is demonstrated well by Tom Hanks in the film *Cast Away*.

In the movie, Tom Hanks (spoiler alert!) plays Chuck Nolan, who is in a plane crash and is marooned on a little island by himself for over four years. In the early months of being stranded, he finds a Wilson brand volleyball that he famously personifies into his only friend on the island. Nolan talks to it, argues with it, reasons with it, and even almost dies trying to rescue it at one point. Yes, a volleyball.

Now, if you haven't seen the movie, summing up that part of the film as I did in just a few sentences probably makes you laugh. However, if you've seen the movie, you know that Wilson the volleyball has truly become Nolan's only friend, and losing it would be tragic. The volleyball is his only sense of connection to humanity and relationship. Without Wilson, he would have gone completely insane.

Like Tom Hanks' character in *Cast Away*, you were not meant to live life alone. You and I need regular emotional, spiritual, and physical connections with people who are genuine because that is the way we were created by God. That is the way the Creator designed it. That is the way the Creator designed you.

We are meant for relationship, so the value we place on connecting with friends in the context of relationship is tantamount to the kind of people we will eventually become. So...who do you want to become?

Ralph Waldo Emerson said, "The only way to have a friend is to be one." Being a good friend is a godly thing. It sets you up for a healthy life that brings glory to Jesus and joy to your soul. You were meant for friendship on various levels, and I believe friendship is one of the most important building blocks on which to base any romantic relationship.

IT IS THE BEST PART

Whenever I get asked what my favorite part of marriage is, I'm able to answer quickly by saying, "My wife is my best friend." That might seem a little boring and cliché to some of you, but I have to say

I'm telling truth. I love the fact that I get to spend the rest of my life with my bestie. Yeah, I just said *bestie.*

Seriously, though, the blessing of being able to enjoy my days and nights with someone I really love *and* really like is a total win. The familiar feelings of romantic puppy love fluctuate as life ebbs and flows in my marriage, but one of the major things I can always come back to with Rachael is the fact that she is my best friend.

I like being around her. I like talking with her. I like sharing inside jokes with her and laughing until we both tear up. I like making fun of her (in a kindhearted way, of course) and she *loves* making fun of me. I want to spend time with her. She's the first person I talk to when a big event happens in my life, and she's the first person I communicate with when something difficult happens to me. Yes, I love my wife, but I also like my wife...because she's my best friend.

Here's why I'm telling you this: if you can't be friends with the person you're interested in dating or currently dating, you probably shouldn't be dating. I know that may sound like a heaping tablespoon of plain common sense, but it is astounding to me how many young couples are attracted to one another in many ways, but they simply aren't that great of friends. Hearing a guy or girl say something like, "I'm not sure if I would want to be friends with this person if we weren't dating," or "We're clicking on all the romantic levels, but we just can't seem to get on the same page as friends," makes me profoundly sad. Friendship can and should be the absolute best part of your dating relationship.

As I mentioned earlier, those romantic feelings you naturally experience when you are interested in someone have a tendency to be very fickle. They are turbo charged when you are young, spurred on by hormones (and maybe Mountain Dew), but they can quickly subside when just a small amount of time passes. Many people place all their chips, so to speak, on the feelings aspect of the relationship, and this is simply unwise to do. Of course feelings are important in any dating relationship, so don't misunderstand what I'm saying here. They are of profound importance when you are involved in a romance. But to live there and only there, hoping the electricity will continue to flow between the two of you in that puppy love kind of way, is foolish.

I remember when things were just getting started between Rachael and me. This little bubble of joy would rise in my throat any time we had some special connection, and I felt the electricity. A flattering comment she would make about me, a message she'd leave for me, a look she would give me, when we would hold hands—all of that stuff made me feel the electricity as we were first dating. But then time passes, and sometimes those things don't make me feel the electricity the way they once did. Does that mean we don't have chemistry anymore or we aren't attracted to one another anymore or that our marriage relationship is doomed? Of course not!

Everyone knows that feelings can be fleeting. The truth is, I feel more connected and more attracted to Rachael now than I ever did back then because our relationship is years and years stronger than it was when we first started dating. The electricity might sometimes be gone in the little things, but the important foundation of friendship is stronger...and we will always work toward making that foundation even more powerful as the years progress in our marriage. To run with the illustration, the electricity is now not in the form of just a little shock because of puppy love feelings—it's a power plant of energy that gets stronger every day.

Placing all the importance of your dating relationship on romantic feelings is dangerous because of its capricious nature, but if you build a solid foundation of friendship in your relationship, it won't matter as much when the feelings come and go because you will know that the foundation is what the connection rests on when your hormones subside (or the caffeine high fades).

WORK IT

Most of the time, friendships begin in a very natural way and they are somewhat easy to maintain if there is a deep connection between two people. But as most of us know, things don't always stay that way. The same goes for dating relationships. In the very wise book of Proverbs, verse 17:17a says:

A friend loves at all times.

As we begin to think of our dating relationship more in terms of a thriving friendship, we will want to engage with the natural work it will take to maintain that friendship. Dating can be hard. Friendship can be hard. And when you put dating and friendship together, those variables can make it doubly difficult! But like anything we think is worth it, we'll work fervently to maintain the relationship. Here's how...

First, you need to be disciplined. If you want to get in shape, you need to commit to a regiment of repeated exercise. If you want to gain muscle mass, you need to methodically hit the gym and lift weights. If you want to drop a few pounds after a season of liberal munching during the holidays, you have to control your diet in the new year. All of these things take discipline. And by definition, discipline is the habitual practice of training yourself to obey a certain code of behavior in order to achieve a particular goal.

Discipline, of course, is not only required for getting in shape or losing weight, it's also necessary when it comes to maintaining the kind of healthy friendship you need in your dating relationship. You need to take the initiative and be intentional about working on your friendship, not see it as just a little extra thing you sustain on the side. If you neglect the friendship element at the beginning of the relationship, you certainly won't work on it when times are difficult and the puppy love has dwindled.

It takes discipline to intentionally communicate with someone when you're tired or busy or it's inconvenient for you, but that's what good friends do. It takes discipline to meet someone for coffee early in the morning when you've been up late the night before for whatever reason, but if you make the commitment, you need to follow through with it because that's what a friend does.

Invest in your friendship now and you will see the fruit of that investment in the future, I promise. Couples who only spend time on the romantic aspect of their relationship have a lot of emotional highs in the initial stages of their dating life, but when tough times happen and things aren't so happy-go-lucky all the time, things can crumble quickly if there isn't any solid foundation beyond the gooey emotions. It's easy to be lovey-dovey, but friendship takes effort, and like most anything that requires discipline, the effort of working at your friendship will pay off in the future.

A guy I know named Chris used to think that romance and friendship didn't pair well, so he never spent any time working on being a good friend to the girls he dated. Sure, he was a romantic and would plan elaborate dates to win the heart of the girl he was pursuing, but his dating relationships never lasted longer than a month or two because he simply wasn't that great of a friend to his girlfriends. When the puppy love inevitably wore off, the girl he was with would break up with him because she would always want more from him than just the romance. Unfortunately, when I last saw him, he still hadn't learned this lesson, and he still didn't have a long lasting relationship.

Secondly, a solid relationship needs something that I like to define as "gumption." Spunk. Oomph. Moxie. Get-up-and-go. Basically, it means being there for the other person when it's hard or inconvenient to be there for the other person.

This applies to more than just the natural obstacles that arise in a relationship because of a certain environment, timing, or outside influence from other people. Yes, we need to be there for our dating partners in those situations, obviously. But the going really gets tough when we find ourselves in a situation that requires us to personally confront a girlfriend or boyfriend. This can mean taking a risk and discussing something difficult because it will ultimately help our partner and build him or her up to be more like Jesus.

Oscar Wilde said, "True friends stab you in the front," meaning we need to talk with our girlfriend or boyfriend about any issues we may see becoming a potential stumbling block toward godly growth instead of succumbing to the temptation of talking behind his or her back. And even more appropriately for Christians, Proverbs 27:6 says,

Wounds from a friend are better than many kisses
from an enemy. (NLT)

I would much rather have a friend say the hard thing and raise the bar as a challenge to the way I live my life, than an enemy pat me on the back via false sentiment. And if the person you're dating isn't the kind of friend who is willing to challenge you to be better, do you really want this person as a dating partner? If you are dating someone who simply agrees with everything you do and isn't willing to move into the tough conversations because he or she simply wants to keep the peace, how will either of you grow?

Or worse, if all you want is a boyfriend or girlfriend who never confronts you about anything because you never want to develop into anything other than what you are right now, you shouldn't be dating. If that describes you, go buy a dog...or a robot...or a robot dog. They'll obey your orders.

One of the best things about bringing other people into our lives is that they challenge us to move into higher levels of maturity. Date someone who has a spine and is willing to help make you a better you.

Now, let me be clear about what I'm saying here and what I'm not saying. I am saying that the person you date should inspire you to grow and walk closer with Jesus. I am not saying that the person you date should be a domineering dictator who constantly tells you how to live your life. There is a line between deep care for someone who encourages you to challenge him to live better, and a manipulative control freak who demands others to conform to her instruction. Many have crossed that line, and when it happens, bad things often follow.

I am not telling you to constantly point out the flaws in your dating partner and demand that he or she get his or her act together. I am not telling you to stand in judgment of your girlfriend's character defects and make her feel small because she isn't perfect. I am not telling you to passive-aggressively mock your boyfriend in order to get him to behave the way you want him to every hour of the day. This kind of motivation for changing someone is just as sinful as the flaws you might see in your partner. No, please don't use what I'm saying as a license to cut down the person you're dating.

It's important that we gently instruct our dating partner to walk with Jesus, but how that instruction is delivered is just as important (if not more so) than the instruction itself. When and if you decide to deliver the wound that Proverbs 27:6 talks about, make sure you put an ample amount of prayer into it and examine your motivations for doing so before you open your mouth and offer your instruction. Yes, the wound can hurt when it's inflicted, but if it is done without the specific purpose of helping the other person grow, irreparable damage can be done.

Think of it like this: you are walking along a city street at night, and you happen upon a person who is lying on the ground. He has been stabbed in the abdomen, and because of the cut, he is bleeding out right there on the pavement. You, being a professionally trained doctor coming home from your rounds at the hospital (did I forget to mention that?) happen to have a battery-powered cauterizer right in your bag that seals open wounds (I know, I know...just go with me on this). Now, you are well aware that the instrument you have in your bag can save the person who's been stabbed from losing too much blood and dying, but you also know that the tool itself, once used without proper anesthetic, can cause a significant amount of pain.

If you choose to just leave the person there on the ground because you don't want to hurt him with your cauterizer any more than he already is, you know your choice would be idiotic. He needs help, and you're the best person for the job.

However, if you pull the cauterizer out of your bag, turn it on, and start to haphazardly carve away at the injured person's gut without any sense of delicacy, you would cause additional injury to the person and those kinds of actions would make you a monster.

But, there is a third choice. You could tell the stabbed person you are a doctor and although what you are about to do will be painful, it is the best way to seal up the wound, stop the bleeding, and consequently save his life. You could then cauterize the stab wound with accuracy, skill, and compassion. Sure, the process would be painful, but the hemorrhaging would stop and the stab wound victim would eventually heal.

Okay, so this little illustration might be a bit graphic for you, but I hope you understand what I'm getting at here. If we see someone bleeding out in some form or fashion, we can ignore it (which is obvious foolishness), we can choose to treat him roughly, which might further injure him, or we can gently try to stop the bleeding because we care. Many times, the boyfriend or girlfriend is the best person for the job because this person is the one who knows the other person well enough to handle the situation with grace, discretion, and accuracy. This person isn't just a boyfriend or girlfriend, he or she is a true friend.

Rachael has done this well as my friend, not only now as my wife, but before we were married and even before we were engaged. She has always been a wonderful example for me of grace and truth, and the Lord has used her to cauterize the areas of bleeding in my life. She has delicately inquired about some of my anger issues, helped me process through my areas of sinful prejudice, and even called me out on my sometimes-present critical attitude. She's a great friend now, and she was a great friend when we were dating. I cherish that aspect of our relationship. She cared for me early on when things were just getting started for us.

Of course, it's never easy for a friend to point out your short-comings (especially when you're trying to impress this person all the time), but real friends do this because they refuse to let you stay where you're at, wallowing in your failures. The veneer of perfection cannot and will not last long in your dating relationship, so let your boyfriend or girlfriend see you, flaws and all.

And just as a side note, serving as an instrument of truth also requires appropriate timing in a romantic relationship. A first date is not the right time to point out someone's issues. Like in a friendship with a member of the same sex, a platform of trust must be built before the liberty of correction can be exercised. Going there too quickly can ruin the friendship and the dating relationship. Use caution and wisdom.

FIRST THINGS FIRST

As we've clearly seen, being a good friend isn't easy. It's messy and awkward and inconvenient. And if you're going to be a good girlfriend or boyfriend, you must, must, must, be a good friend first. Strong and godly friendship is the hinge on which the door of your relationship swings. Make sure that hinge is sturdy and well attended to. If so, it will set you up for a bright future that honors Christ, and it will be a shining example others can look to in this world of broken relationships.

In his gospel, John wrote:

*Greater love has no one than this, that someone lay down his life
for his friends. (John 15:13)*

Friendship is about giving, not taking, and the same should be
true of dating. Sure it's hard, but dating should be about thinking of
the other person's needs first instead of looking for him or her to
continually serve us. Again, remember Emerson who said, "The only
way to have a friend is to be one."

This is the sentiment each of us should strive for. If we do, God
will be glorified in our relationships, the relationships themselves will
be more fulfilling, fewer breakups will happen, and the breakup process
will be much more civil because friendships will matter.

GROUND CONTROL:
THE DARK ART OF MANIPULATION

I distinctly remember Driver's Education class during my sophomore year of high school like it was many years ago...because it was. Nevertheless, I still remember it well.

The head football coach was my Driver's Ed teacher, and although that might seem like a bad thing, it wasn't. It was actually a good thing. Coach Ragsdale was his name, and he was a laid-back southern gentleman who sounded a lot like Matthew McConaughey in any movie set below the Mason-Dixon Line. I liked Coach Ragsdale, and the truth is he was probably the perfect faculty member to teach Driver's Ed because of his skill at making everyone else around him feel at ease; this is a quality that is quite valuable when teaching fifteen-year-olds how to not crash cars into trees and/or trash cans.

The reason that time was so memorable was not because of the in-class lessons Coach Ragsdale taught, but because of our in-the-car times out on the real streets behind the wheel. When you are fifteen and somebody tells you she loves you, you're gonna believe it, but when you're fifteen, sitting in class, and somebody tells you you'll be driving a car that day, you're gonna pee a little in your pants from excitement.

I loved nearly everything about those glorious times in the "Student Driver" labeled Dodge Stratus, weaving my way through orange cones during what Coach called "warm up driving," and then moving on to the "workout" which consisted of taking the four-door sedan onto the highway. It was so freeing to finally be able to drive a real car after years of watching my parents do it.

The only thing that bothered me about our time on the road, however, was the uniqueness of the particular Dodge Stratus we were privileged to operate. See, this was one of those specially modified cars that had an additional brake pedal on the passenger side floorboard, the kind the driving instructor had easy access to. Yep, whenever Coach Ragsdale wanted to usurp my driving freedom and apply the brakes to end my reign of careless gas pedal compression, he could. And I didn't like that.

If we were out in the special car, I would have a blast learning how to drive until I remembered that I wasn't really driving with the kind of freedom I craved. Coach could literally stop the car any time he deemed necessary, and that made me feel like I wasn't really in complete control of the car. I didn't want him to exercise his right to govern my street-racer cravings, but he could step on that pedal any time he wanted to and end my attempts to go faster.

Even now, as I think about those Driver's Ed days from my past, I can't help but notice the same feelings I experience today when I crave control over my life as a whole. I want to have full control over every aspect of my existence, without interruption from anyone or anything that might steal that jurisdiction away from me. And when the control I crave is threatened, my grip on things gets tighter and tighter in my attempt to reclaim what I believe should be mine: government over my own life. And my guess is you are probably the same way.

Nearly everyone sinfully loves the idea of having authority and power over the world around them. Each of us clamors for some semblance of order over our environment, and the proof of that lies in how people respond when control is stripped away from them— they usually freak out. Don't believe me? Just try going to a grocery store in South Carolina to buy milk when a rare snowstorm is about to hit. Not only will all the milk be gone, but most of the shelves will be empty, and there will probably be some kind of mini-riot in the bread aisle because people in the south generally believe a light dusting of snow means the apocalypse is about to begin.

See what I mean? We love control. We crave it. We're addicted to it. And when we think we might lose it, our sanity crumbles. What does all this have to do with dating and relationships, you might ask? Everything.

Along with our desire to govern our own lives, each of us also has the sinful tendency to exert control over the person we might be dating. In our flawed minds, we think of this as wise guidance for our special friend so he or she can benefit from our benevolent decision-making, but in the real world, it's called manipulation.

Now, we've already talked about this a bit in the chapter on com-munication, specifically in relation to our desire to play games with the one we're interested in (or not interested in) for the sole purpose of entertaining ourselves when we lack maturity. And of course, all those principles I mentioned in that chapter still apply here, but what I want to do is go a layer deeper into the dark art of manipulation and address a few specifics on its destructive qualities in dating relationships.

TRUST ME

If someone is a manipulator, it implies there might be a few things going on behind the scenes that have led to the person unofficially wearing the title. Of course, no one would probably ever self-identify as a manipulator because the moniker comes with negative connota-tions. Regardless, there are certain people who just are manipulators.

Quite often when I hear the word 'manipulator,' I think of a per-son who schemes in the shadows, wearing an evil smile as he steeple his fingers and plots the demise of other people's well-being. This is certainly not always true, but as cartoonish as this mental image might seem, it still rests on the idea that being a manipulator is not a good thing. The sad truth is that each and every one of us wrestles with manipulation in our lives from time to time.

I certainly have. I've often caught myself saying or doing little things in order to purposefully ignite a reaction in someone else. Back in college, there was a season when my roommate and I used to intentionally call ourselves ugly in front of girls just to be funny. Truthfully, I just wanted the girls to disagree with me so I could feel better about myself and garner some sort of reaction out of them.

When I said I was ugly, my true motivations were surprising and subtle because I didn't really dig deeper into the reasons for my manipulation until a friend of mine called me on it. She literally smacked me on the arm one evening and told me to stop saying what I was saying because she knew what I was attempting to do. It was a wake-up call for me, and I consequently became more cautious about the kind of joking I did. Manipulation can be a dark art that is embedded into our regular behavior, and it's important that we cut it out of our lifestyle because it is poisonous for both us and the relationships we are in.

Plain and simple, when we want to manipulate, we want to control things. Why? Well, there could be many driving factors, but my bet is that when things boil down to the most basic reason, we find that people who struggle with consistent manipulation of others have a lot of trouble with trust.

Naturally, when you trust someone, it means that you place your faith in that person. And although we talk about being faithful in Christian circles, it's actually something we don't do very much. We have trouble trusting God and others, so the void often gets filled with our feeble attempts at trying to control the Creator of the universe, while at the same time trying to manipulate the people around us. We do this because we think that if we are in the driver's seat of our lives, we can steer it in any direction we wish. This is a comforting thing. It protects us from injury.

If someone is in the habit of regularly trying to control people, dangerous tactics of manipulation frequently get pulled into his or her dating relationships as well, and when this happens, things can get completely ugly, fairly quickly. People don't want to be a pup-pet, especially if they think they are being controlled by the person they're romantically involved with, but the dark art of manipulation is a frequent problem between couples. Remember, manipulation is the fruit of a lack of trust, and although a boyfriend or girlfriend may not have given his or her dating partner any reason to be distrustful, the seeds of uncertainty can come from a deep place in the person's history, causing problems in the present. Quite often, manipulation from a dating partner is simply the default because he or she has been burned in the past by a previous romantic partner. Control might be the only way this person feels protected from getting hurt again.

I'm not a psychologist, but I have worked with a number of people over the years who have confided in me about their relationship woes. Sadly, there are many young people who walk around injured from a crappy relationship history, and the thought of freely trusting someone again within the world of romance is overwhelming. So much so that they don't even know how to engage with someone in a healthy way, free of manipulation.

If I have just described you or someone you know, don't be discouraged—there is hope! If we are ever going to be able to trust other people fully, we must first start with trusting the One who created us. It begins here. If your relationship with God isn't right, no other friendship or romantic relationship will be fully right either. When we are able to engage freely with God and trust Him because we believe He is good and He loves us, our other earthly relationships will flow directly from the most important one. If our perspective on God keeps us focused on the truth that our Father wants what is best for us (in spite of our circumstances), we will be able to experience deep intimacy with Him, and this gives us the freedom to release our control of those around us.

We will believe Him when He says,

For God so loved the world that he gave his one and only Son, that whoever believes in him shall not perish but have eternal life. (John 3:16)

and

Greater love has no one than this: to lay down one's life for one's friends. (John 15:13)

and

But God demonstrates his own love for us in this: While we were still sinners, Christ died for us. (Romans 5:8)

We'll believe these Scriptures, meditate on them, and build a foundation of trust in the Lord because we know He loves us. He loves us so much that He voluntarily died for us...there is no greater love than dying for someone (John 15:13). And as we begin to truly believe this to our core, intimacy will develop because intimacy is a product of what we believe or don't believe about someone. If we believe the truth about Jesus and His sacrifice for each one of us individually, we will develop strong bonding roots in our relationship with Him that will naturally bleed over into our human relationships with others.

Sure, it's hard to trust other people, especially when your heart is on the line in romance. Getting hurt in your love life stings worse than anything else. It can shake you to your soul and leave lasting scars of doubt and pain and suspiciousness of others. But as we begin to trust God in a vulnerable and honest way, He will help heal the scars of past relationship wounds, and the temptation to mistrust, control, and manipulate others will dwindle in light of the healthier foundation we have built upon Jesus Christ.

He is the healer of all things, and He can heal you...if you let Him. Get right with Him by taking the free gift He offers to you. Each of us tries to be our own savior by picking a path that leads to ruin. We all think we know what is best for us, and that is why we are born to be rebels. We all turn our backs on God and go our own way because we think we've got it all figured out. We substitute purity with poison and drink deeply from the unwashed cup it rests in.

And although we are condemned to eternal death because of our rebellion, God still chooses to move toward us by absorbing our deserved punishment Himself in the person of Jesus Christ. The solution has presented itself quite clearly, and every person in the world is faced with a choice: personally receive the punishment for our own defiance, or let Him do it. The price has to be paid.

Those who humble themselves and take the gift that God offers become children of God and they no longer bear the burden of eternal condemnation (Romans 8:1). But the glorious reward God offers in Jesus is not just a ticket to glory, it is the beginning of a relationship unlike any other. It is a personal relationship with our Maker, built upon true love, trust, intimacy, tenderness, and care. Eternity with God begins the day we make the decision to receive what He has offered, and when we take it, He begins the good work of healing us from within. Then and only then are we able to build truly healthy romantic relationships with solid foundations.

A relationship with God is built on this fundamental point of trust, and if you've never made that decision to receive it, what better time is there than right now? As I've said, all other important relationships in life should be assembled on the basis of this most important one, so I'd recommend you start in the right place.

I hope you understand what I'm trying to say here. The greatest example in my life of a loving relationship is not the one I have with my wife (although that one's magnificent), but the one I have with my Savior. Jesus, and Jesus alone, is the foundation upon which Rachael and I have been able to build our marriage. We understand that without a genuine relationship with Him first, everything else would be constructed with shoddy materials. And because we both know this, we are able to love each other more intimately. We trust one another in spite of our obvious sin, and we are able to forgive one another when we fail.

Our insecurities don't have to give definition to our character. We can choose to relinquish control over our lives to our loving Heavenly Father, and we can ask Him to give us direction and wisdom as we go about building friendships and romantic relationships with other people.

Just as God used my friend that evening back in college to smack my perspective back into alignment so I would stop trying to manipulate a reaction out of girls by calling myself "ugly," God can also use any means to reprogram our hearts away from manipulation. A proper understanding of His love and sacrifice for us, revealed in the Scriptures, can mold any control freak like me into a more Christ-honoring person.

If your default mode with a boyfriend or girlfriend is to control via manipulation, ask yourself why you are struggling with trust and allow God to place His finger on the area of your heart that might need some attention. Jesus is in the business of changing lives. He always has been, and He can do the good work of transforming you to be more like Him. This, in turn, will make your romantic relationships improve exponentially. All you have to do is ask Him to get involved and trust that He'll follow through with His promises.

And He will...trust me.

SINGLENESS IS NOT A CURSE

When I was younger, my single friends and I would constantly be told that singleness was a gift, and if you look through the Bible, there are places like 1 Corinthians 7:6-9 that say,

> *Now as a concession, not a command, I say this. I wish that all were as I myself am. But each has his own gift from God, one of one kind and one of another. To the unmarried and the widows I say that it is good for them to remain single as I am. But if they cannot exercise self-control, they should marry. For it is better to marry than to burn with passion.*

Of course, after being told by church folk that being single, like the Apostle Paul, is a gift, we all inevitably joked about wanting to return the gift. Singleness a gift? Who in the world thinks that single-ness should be something that is considered a blessing to be desired? Especially when you're young and full of hormones? Wow. Talk about not knowing your audience.

And as the years rolled by, I continued to receive the gift of singleness from the Lord. Every year for Christmas, Easter, my birthday, the 4th of July, and Valentine's Day, it was the exact same gift—singleness. It's kind of like getting dress socks as your big present from your parents every year at Christmas time...sad and extremely disappointing. Why on earth would God continue to "bless" me with singleness when all I wanted was to share my life with a godly woman? Didn't the Lord understand that my motives weren't simply self-concerning, but also to heap more glory upon His good name? Marriage does that, right? Yet I remained single for much longer than I wanted to.

Of course, the proverbial carrot of marriage was dangled in front of my face a time or two, mostly with a pretty young woman named Amy who I met on a missions project, of all places. She seemed to be the perfect match for me at first: she loved Jesus, she wanted to be a full-time missionary like me, she had a great personality, and she thought I was funny. Not much more to ask for than that. We began dating near the end of the project, and even though our relationship was long-distance, we were making it work. We talked frequently on the phone, I flew out to see her when our schedules aligned, and we both did our best to encourage one another despite the distance.

But the day arrived when the relationship came to an end and she broke up with me. No, I won't lie and say it was a mutual decision. She ended it, and I was a mess. I allowed my heart and mind to become too attached to her and the idea of spending our lives together, so when she broke up with me, I kind-of lost it. The gift of singleness was once again delivered to my doorstep, and I was heartbroken.

I couldn't bring myself to believe that I was meant to be single forever because I wanted a wife so badly. God had to know that about me, yet here I was, without someone. Eventually I did get over Amy, and I even dated a few more girls before my wife, Rachael, came into my life. But I believe I made one fundamental mistake that poisoned the well of my single years—those years that lasted until I got married at age twenty-nine. I believed that singleness was a curse. As much as I wanted to trust that being unattached to someone was a blessing from God, I simply had too much trouble believing that concept in my heart.

When everything inside you screams for a deep romantic connection with another person, it's hard to listen to anything else, no matter how true or wise it may be. I wanted to be loved. I wanted to be wanted. I would literally ask myself, *What's the matter with you? Are you unloveable? Why doesn't anybody want you? Why won't anyone love you?*

I WANT YOU TO WANT ME

I'm short. I am. In comparison to the average American male, I'm well below the curve of what a normal dude is supposed to be, height-wise. By the time I finished puberty in late high school (yes, you read that right: *late* high school) and stopped growing, I had only sprouted to a meager 5'6", and all through my adolescent years, I was labeled as "cute." Now cute might seem like a good thing on the surface, but it's actually not. When you call something cute, you're kind of talking down to it like it's a puppy or an American Girl doll, so when girls would say that I was cute, I knew they were really saying, "I want to ruffle your hair, give you a juice box, and pinch your nose." Needless to say, I got sick of being cute.

All of this came to a head in the middle of my sophomore year of college. I was having a conversation with this girl outside one of the academic buildings on campus, and I said something that made her laugh. After she finished laughing, she pointed at me and said, "You know, Shelby, you are so cute."

This was the breaking point for me. I'd had enough, so I pushed her pointing finger away from my face, looked her right in the eye, and said, "Listen to me. I've been cute for twenty years, and I'm done. I do not want to be cute anymore! What is it with you women? Why can't I just be...*desirable*?"

I think I said the word *desirable* with a little too much angst in my voice because that girl pretty much avoided me for the rest of our time together at college. Oh well...life goes on.

The reason I'm telling you this story is to help you understand that there was a history behind my belief system when I was single. I believed that a woman would never really take me seriously as a man because I wasn't actually desirable. I was cute and not a real option for any self-respecting female. Consequently, I believed there was something wrong with me that made me unloveable and single.

IS SINGLE BAD OR GOOD?

We've all got our scars. Whether it's a mean-spirited name that someone called us in middle school or something that happened to us involving betrayal by a friend we trusted. We've all been hurt in some form or fashion, leading us to walk around with the damage well into our later years. And if that damage happens to be in the area of romance, the scars can last twice as long, leaving us with an improper view of singleness and what it actually means.

If we think of being single as a bad thing, as though there is something wrong with us or because we're being punished for failing in a relationship, we start to view it from a negative angle. For many years, I believed that I was single because I was never good enough, man enough, or tall enough to be seriously considered by any woman out there.

There's a fundamental flaw in this kind of thinking. We are looking at singleness as a punishment or a substandard way of life that needs to be fixed so that we can finally be truly fulfilled and happy. This kind of thinking leads to a defective emotional foundation which in turn underscores the false belief that singleness is a curse that needs to be lifted. We may continue in this thought pattern and imagine that if the curse is lifted all of our problems will go away. I even remember joking about this and saying something like, "Deep down, I know that marriage won't solve all my problems...but even deeper down than that, I believe marriage will solve all my problems."

I bought into the idea that being single means being half a person, unable to live fully without the other half who is out there some-where, just for me. As I approached my mid-twenties, all of my other friends were getting married and having their first round of kids. People started to pity me, so they kept trying to connect me with "someone I think you'd like." Some family friends even asked, "Do you think you might be gay? Is that why you haven't found anyone?"

When I was asked this question by people I had known for nearly my whole life, I couldn't help but think to myself, "Is being single really that bad? Why is everyone treating me like I have this disease that needs to be cured?" And with this thought came a new paradigm on my view of singleness.

I had been treating my single life as this wound that was preventing me from thriving as a person, when in reality, singleness was potentially a great opportunity for me. I had been thinking that I needed a wife in order to be whole, when the truth was that Jesus had already made me whole by coming into my life and saving me from my sin.

A friend of mine from The Gospel Coalition, Matt Smethurst, says it this way:

> The most fully human and complete person ever to live was single. Marriage is not ultimate. Jesus is ultimate.[12]

True. For so long, I sincerely believed I was like a human puzzle with a piece missing. I thought that if I found a wife, my puzzle would be complete and the hole in my life would be filled, making my picture joyful, beautiful, and complete. But where in Scripture does it say that a spouse will do all of those things? Yes, the Bible does say that if a man finds a wife, he finds a good thing (Proverbs 18:22), but that good thing was never meant to be the ultimate thing. The only truly ultimate relationship that can satisfy any deep human desire for a knowing connection is a relationship with Jesus Christ. I had Him in my life already, and I was neglecting Him in my search for a woman.

I believe that many followers of Jesus who are single suffer from the same problem that I did because they are in search of the same thing I was. My life changed when I came to realize that no one person would ever be able to love me the way that God already did. No dating relationship would ever be able to fill the self-created void I thought I had in my heart. Yes, I wanted to be loved, but I didn't realize that I was already being loved. It took me too long to see this, but once I finally did, I began to experience freedom *within* my singleness, not *in spite* of it.

RELATIONSHIP STATUS

Society has taught us that we must be in a romantic relationship with someone in order to prove that we have value. If we are single, there's something wrong with us: we're too picky, we're a loser, or we need to be fixed. The culture around us drives home this way of thinking, and it has naturally bled over into Christianity.

Our churches today seem puzzled over what to do with singles. If people aren't married, they are put together in little social groups based on the idea that they'll fall in love and marry one another, and this will make everyone more comfortable. Rarely do you see a church that blends marrieds and singles together in a way that doesn't make singles feel like they're a project to be solved. And God forbid you approach your thirties as a single and regularly attend church.

A female friend of mine in her late thirties told me that she sometimes dreads going to church on Sundays because she consistently gets asked if she's dating anyone yet. In fact, one Sunday, an older woman in the church struck up a conversation with my friend and asked her if she struggled with lesbianism. After a look of shock fell over my friend's face, the older woman said she meant no offense, but suggested that if my friend "dressed to impress" a bit more, maybe she'd find a husband.

The problem with viewing singleness negatively isn't just within our own hearts, it's the pervasive opinion held by our society and Christian culture alike. The pressure hits from both sides, and all of this negativity gathers, contributing to feelings of deficiency for those who are single. And the clock keeps ticking.

SINGLENESS AND PURITY

In her book, *Sex and the Single Christian Girl: Fighting for Purity in a Rom-Com World*, Marion Jordan Ellis says, "A wedding ring does not make a woman immune to spiritual darkness."[13] And although we read a quote like this and nod along with enthusiastic agreement, we still secretly think that marriage is the solution for the "purity problem."

Yes, the Bible is clear on issues of lust and the need to resist it. It even goes so far as to say:

But if they cannot control themselves, they should marry, for it is better to marry than to burn with passion. (1 Corinthians 7:9)

But this is a calling for a specific problem. I've never said to a guy, "You struggled with internet pornography last night? You need to get married today to solve that problem!" 1 Corinthians 7 is addressing a pattern in someone's life, not individualized solutions for broad-based sin.

Marion Jordan Ellis brings to light something that is worth exploring. She addresses the underlying belief that taking marriage vows erases the sinful root of lust and impurity within someone's heart. It doesn't, and the quicker you realize this, the better. When someone puts on a wedding ring, he or she doesn't immediately become bulletproof to the sin of lust and sexual impurity. Sure, there is an outlet within the marriage relationship, but if the seed of contamination still remains, so will the eventual sprouting of sin from the seed. Once again, we discover that behavior modification is not the key to the Christian life. The gospel is.

But when it is communicated to single people (either intentionally or unintentionally) that marriage will provide the solution to the purity problem, we are pointing not to the gospel as the remedy, but to behavior modification.

"Ooo, if you could just hold out until you get married, then you'll finally be able to have sex and you won't struggle with impurity anymore!" How does a statement like this align with the biblical perspective regarding sin? In essence, this statement is saying, "just stop it" until you are allowed to "go ahead." It gives singles the false expectation that their hope should rest in marriage.

But our hope for purity (or anything that is glorifying) is not in marriage—our hope is in heaven. The finish line isn't the night after you say your wedding vows; the finish line is when you meet Jesus face-to-face and you no longer need to wrestle with any kind of sinful desire, failure, or impurity.

This perspective is imperative as we address issues of sexual impurity because communicating that the marriage bed will make everything better is simply devastating for men and women who struggle with same sex attraction (SSA). If we want to have any kind of godly presence or witness in the lesbian, bisexual, gay, transgender, and questioning (LBGTQ) community, we cannot say that the solutions to sexual problems are found in traditional marriage. This is simply not true.

Opening ears and hearts to Jesus in our culture comes from communicating the truth of the Bible with our words *and* our lives. And the truth is that we are all sexual rebels needing to be clothed in the unflinching fidelity of Christ. No one has ever gone to heaven for being heterosexual, so we must stop communicating the false idea that acting a certain way will get someone right with God. It won't— only Jesus will.

POWER TO THE PEOPLE

You can't fix sexual impurity when you're single by trying harder to be more pure, and you can't fix sexual impurity *within a marriage* by trying harder to be more pure. Jesus, and Jesus alone, is the solution to our purity problems, regardless of our relationship status. Each of us needs to not only preach this to ourselves so that we might experience freedom from sexual sin, but also preach it to others who wrestle with sexual sin. So, the Sunday School answer here is familiar: Jesus. But what does this really mean?

In my early Christian years, I understood in theory what people meant when they said that Jesus is the solution to the various problems I had, but I didn't really get how that played out in my day-to-day life. "Okay," I would think, "I understand that I shouldn't just buckle down and try harder to be better. I need the gospel to transform me from within in order to see real life change. So...what do I do now?"

That's a fair question that I think a lot of people are asking when we tell them to allow the gospel to change their lives. People want to experience the change that comes with letting Jesus work in their hearts, but they probably need a little more to go on than just, "Pray and read your Bible."

When it comes to the very common and difficult problem of sexual impurity, we simply lack the power to see victory on a continuous basis. We are like an elaborate and beautifully constructed house with every amenity you can think of...but the electricity has been shut off.

No doubt you've experienced a power outage before. These can be quite common if you live in an area of the world that is no stranger to fierce lightning storms in the summer or dangerous ice storms in the winter. When the power goes out (especially in the winter), it feels as though your entire world has shut down. There's no light, no heat, no refrigeration for your food, no charging of the battery on your computer. Your home becomes a cold (literally), empty shell of what it once was without electricity because it was never built to operate without power. The same goes for us.

Trying harder to be a pure person is simply impossible. We lack the power to make this happen because we are frail and feeble when we try to go toe-to-toe against the behemoth that is sexual sin. On our own, it cannot be done...but *with God* all things are possible.

When someone accepts the free gift that God offers in the sacrifice of His Son, Jesus Christ, that person enters into a relationship with Him, and the third Person of the Trinity comes to dwell inside—the Holy Spirit. God, the Holy Spirit, is the electricity that makes a house run properly. He gives us the power to experience victory over sexual sin in ways that never would be possible on our own. And because He lives inside each and every believer when we say "yes" to the gift of Jesus, we can tap into this power any time we want to in order to see success.

It all happens by faith. We access the power that the Holy Spirit offers by asking Him to do the work of Christ within us and then trusting that He'll do what He promised. Many followers of Jesus try to live the Christian life in their own power, and this leads to frustration, anger, and eventually defeat. Trying to "just be better" or "wait until you get married" or "stop it" to experience success in your walk with God will lead to defeat. When you come into a relationship with God, it is by faith, and in the same way, you live the Christian life by faith. Ultimate freedom from sexual sin comes through ongoing surrender to Jesus, and this can only be done by faith.

Through *faith*.

As Christians, we trust God to work in us and bring life to the dead areas of our lives. And even though buckling down and trying harder isn't the answer, we ourselves do, in fact, have a role in cultivating the Spirit's influence. God calls each of us to "fan into flame" the Spirit's power and influence. Here's a biblical example of this:

> *...addressing one another in psalms and hymns and spiritual songs, singing and making melody to the Lord with your heart, giving thanks always and for everything to God the Father in the name of our Lord Jesus Christ, submitting to one another out of reverence for Christ. (Ephesians 5:19-21)*

Like any living space, the heart has an ambiance all its own, and what Paul describes here is an atmosphere of the heart that fosters the greatest influence of the Spirit. This is the experiential reality of the Kingdom of God living and laughing in our hearts, but it's an atmosphere that must be created, almost like a party we have to throw each day.

These are the mechanisms of spiritual transformation—praising, thanking, worshipping, singing, fellowshipping—because these are the elements of a party. And this "party" plays host to the presence of God, filling us with His Spirit, and the Spirit's filling is what transforms us.

Understanding and living this out will change your life. It changed mine. Although this is still a continual struggle, finally grasping what it meant to live a victorious Christian life was the light that broke through the darkness for me. It wasn't about trying to be better, and it wasn't even about longing for my wedding night so that I'd finally be free of sexual sin. It was about allowing the Spirit of God to work in my life right now, so that He could usher in triumph where there was once only defeat.

OPPORTUNITY KNOCKS

With all of its challenges, singleness is not a bad thing, and I wish I had seen that during my single years. If you are single now, I hope you don't think of it as a curse, like I did. The finish line isn't the end of singleness...the finish line is Heaven. Understanding this will free you up to live in a way that brings glory to the name of Jesus.

Singleness can be an opportunity if you let it flourish rather than wish it away. God can do wonderful things during this time in your life. As a single person, you are not responsible for someone else emotionally, financially, or spiritually. You probably don't have a mortgage or kids or increased responsibilities. You are uniquely free to pursue new things.

If you want to, you can pick up and go to Australia for two weeks in the winter (because it's summertime there!) and not worry about whether it will fit into another person's schedule. As a single, you can seek wise counsel, pray, and proceed! There is a fresh simplicity in being single, while marriage brings with it a certain amount of complexity.

If you believe that you constantly need a significant other to be complete or joyful, then ask yourself why you're always hoping for something that you don't have in order to feel satisfied instead of looking to the true fulfillment of a relationship with God through Jesus Christ. He alone satisfies.

Being single does not mean that there is something wrong with you. I hope you understand this, and I hope you believe that single-ness is a gift worth cherishing because once it's gone, it's gone.

My single days are now over, and I miss them sometimes because of the freedom I had to make choices on the fly. I'm not saying that I regret anything about my marriage—not at all. My marriage is lovelier than I could have possibly dreamed. I am saying, however, that I wish I would have appreciated singleness when I had it and not constantly wished it away.

Value and treasure the precious time of your single years for what they are—a loving gift from your Heavenly Father.

SOCIAL (LY AWKWARD) MEDIA

In a recent interview with *Real Simple* magazine, psychologist Sherry Turkle was asked a series of questions about technology and its direct correlation to social interaction. One particular insight she gave made me pause and think about how technology is influencing men and women in the dating pool. When asked why texting has become more common than talking, Sherry Turkle said,

> *Because it protects people from the possibility of confrontation. There's a whole generation that isn't learning how to have a conversation. I asked some kids why they choose to avoid face-*

to-face communication, and one boy said, "It takes place in real time, and you can't control what you're going to say." Without this skill, kids aren't prepared to negotiate many of life's bumps.[14]

Not only kids, I would add, but the young dating generation out there right now.

But before we dive into this chapter, please understand that I'm pro-technology. I have quite a few mobile devices, and I genuinely like how simple they can make my life. I'm not going to spout off a bunch of curmudgeonly statements about how kids these days don't appreciate how easy they've got it and how hard it was for me when "I was their age." Fear not.

However, even as I hold my iPhone, I am deeply passionate about concrete, face-to-face communication. Yes, I love technology, but I don't love how it can erode our ability to connect with one another in a genuine way. As usual, sinful people turn good things into bad things.

TEXTING AND FOMO

Actor and comedian Louis C.K. made headlines after he was interviewed on Conan O'Brien's talk show because of his opinions on the subject of cell phones for kids. C.K. said that he didn't want to get a cell phone for his daughter because he believes mobile devices shape kids into people without empathy or even the ability to have eye contact with someone else. He went on to say,

Underneath everything in your life, there's that thing...that forever empty knowledge that you're alone. Life is tremendously sad, and that's why people text and drive...because they don't

want to be alone for one second.

Louis C.K. makes the point that people are essentially medicating themselves with cell phone usage, trying to avoid any bit of sadness, even a moment. They would rather risk their own life by texting-while-driving than feel alone for even a second.

Of course, all of this was said in the format of a mini stand-up comedy routine, but principally, I think he's on to something here. People are afraid of being alone. The familiar acronym, *FOMO* (Fear Of Missing Out) is the common reality of nearly everyone these days, and it is affecting the way we do life. This fear has shaped the way we communicate, the way we spend our work and free time, the way we acquire information, and the way we socialize with one another romantically.

Both Louis C.K. and psychologist Sherry Turkle have acknowledged that technology has altered the landscape of how people interact with one another, and they would probably both agree that if we aren't careful, technology could damage our ability to move through the necessary processes of sadness and confrontation in a healthy way. It has become especially problematic in relation to communication, thus creating a significant challenge for many singles in the dating world. The interconnectivity that technology promises isn't overly satisfying because of the ways we have chosen to utilize it.

And yes, I am guilty of contributing to the problem, too. I've succumbed many times to the siren call of diving into my pocket for my phone when I've got a few seconds of alone time. It's like a knee-jerk reaction for me. If I'm sitting in the doctor's office waiting room, I grab my phone. If I'm on any form of public transportation, I grab my phone. If I'm just the least bit bored, I grab my phone. And I would guess that you're probably the same way.

Aziz Ansari (another actor and comedian) has a comedy bit about how cell phones and texting have basically ruined the dating scene today. He likens it to, "being a secretary for a really shoddy organization, scheduling the dumbest [stuff] with the flakiest people ever."

Why? Because the rules of the game have changed with texting. Anyone and everyone now has a digital layer of protection, and people don't have to commit to anything. Texting is essentially talking *at* people instead of talking *with* people. When your communication relies solely on the basis of texting, you really feel no sense of accountability or responsibility to anyone, giving you the freedom to walk all over people or ignore them completely. I would agree with Ansari—texting has flattened and dumbed down dating in significant ways.

THE DIGITAL SHEILD

When you get to the guts of it, the problem isn't technology; the problem is what technology has forced to the surface: fear, laziness, apathy, and a desire for control. Naturally, these kinds of sin struggles are already present, perhaps especially when it comes to interacting with the opposite sex. So when the variable of the digital shield is added to the mix, things might seem to be better at first, but when all is said and done, they are actually worse. Let me explain.

It's difficult for a guy to look a girl in the eye and ask her to go out on a date when feelings, nerves, and a sensitive heart is on the line. And I'm sure it's uncomfortably awkward for a girl to tell a guy that she has no desire to be more than friends when he shows obvious interest in a romantic relationship. For both sides of the equation, face-to-face relational tension can be almost unbearable, so if something like a text message can be sent from the safety and comfort of life behind a cell phone, more often than not, the involved parties will opt for it. Then any problems regarding feelings, nerves, or a sensitive heart are solved, right? Hmm, not exactly.

Communication through the digital shield, while solving the problem of initial awkwardness, actually creates an entirely new set of problems far greater than the first. Why? Because a precedent has been set that important communication between this particular guy and girl is going to be dealt with in the easiest way possible...a way that brings the least amount of anxiety, but in effect, glosses over the realities of life. A couple shouldn't be in the habit of retreating to the safety of their phones or computers in times when it's hard to handle the bumps of relationship friction.

I think it was Dumbledore who once said, "Dark and difficult times lie ahead. Soon we must all choose between what is right...and what is easy" (*Harry Potter and The Goblet of Fire*)[15].

Yes, it might be silly to quote Dumbledore in the context of dating, but what he has to say is very true. It's easy to shield yourself from the danger of heartache in a relationship by communicating through technology instead of face-to-face, but that doesn't mean it's right. It's important for us to respect one another enough to spend the time and effort it takes to engage with another person in the flesh, look the other person in the eye, and talk about the important things.

Handling personal issues over a text message, a social media conversation, or even an email when it can be done face-to-face implies retreat. It implies a lack of initiative, and as we went over in the beginning of this chapter, it implies a selfish desire for control.

TO THE MEN

Now, let me take a moment here and talk solely to the men: have face-to-face conversations with women you are interested in. First, you need to rethink your strategy if your idea of asking a girl out is typing a text message to her that says, "Hey, wanna hang out sometime this weekend?" I have talked to many women who have said they wished that a guy would have enough guts to talk with her face-to-face, have a plan about what he'd like to do during an evening of encouragement, and ask her to join him.

Instead, women commonly get a series of lazy text messages from guys who passively hint at the idea they'd like to hang out, saying "maybe you should join me," and the ladies are sick of it. Have a plan, have some guts, and talk to the girl eye-to-eye.

Second, if you go to pick up a girl where she lives, don't pull into the driveway or parking lot and send her a text message that says, "Here." Park the car, get out of the car, have the courtesy to physically walk up to her door, ring the doorbell, meet her roommates or parents, usher her back to your car, open her door for her, and be a gentleman. How cowardly is it when a dude won't even get out of the car to meet a woman's friends or family? You're not going to win any points with the people closest to your date if you hide in your car behind your phone, trust me.

Be a man and step into the social anxiety of meeting people you may not be initially comfortable with. It shows respect for her friends/family, and it communicates you care about every part of her life. When the day comes that my daughters start to date (God help me), if the boy she wants to go out with doesn't have the decency to walk to my door, shake my hand, and engage in a little chitchat with me before he takes her out, he doesn't get to take my daughter out. It's as simple as that.

The girl you might like is already loved by many people in her life, so take the time to meet those people and communicate that you intend to build that girl up, not remain a mystery. Mysterious boys might be appealing to some girls, but let me tell you, I am not impressed. I want my daughters to date boys who live with integrity in the light, not boys who might use my daughters and hide in the shadows behind the privacy of their phones and computer.

And last, I'm not an idiot. I get the way the world works today. I know that a majority of flirting and conversation happens digitally between single people.

"Who asks a girl out face-to-face these days?" Ideally, *you*. Instead of succumbing to the social norms of passive, digital relational interaction, set a different kind of standard by caring for a woman and actually communicating with her personally! Not only will you stand out as a man among boys, it will also communicate care, respect, and character in a world that devalues these admirable traits in men. This is the kind of guy I would trust with my daughters.

TO THE WOMEN

Recently I was driving to work, listening to a secular radio program, and the DJs were talking about the role social media plays in what they called "hook-ups and break-ups." One of the interns at the radio station had just been broken up with, so the DJs on the program were grilling her with questions about how it happened. They also wanted to know what kinds of things she did online after the break up occurred.

The newly single girl said she immediately went to social media and stalked him. She found a message he had posted that stated he was listening to a certain album all day after their breakup. She proceeded to look up the album and go through all the lyrics to every single song, line by line. Eventually, she found a song with references to heartbreak. What she wanted to know was whether the other DJs thought it meant something. Was he as heartbroken as she was? Everyone on the radio program agreed that it probably meant something, and the ex-boyfriend was mourning the breakup just as much as she was.

But as I listened, I thought to myself, *Uh, no it doesn't. They have no idea what it meant. The post that ex-boyfriend made could have meant something totally different, or even nothing at all other than the fact that he liked a particular album.* But of course my opinion didn't matter. Everyone in the studio was certain that it meant something. I'm sure that the group consensus made the broken-up-with girl feel better, but the whole conversation was telling.

Let's start with this, ladies: there is tremendous danger in ascribing specific meaning to online posts when you don't know for sure what the intentions were of the one who posted. It can be very easy to travel down a certain mental road when you read something that's been typed by a guy; however, jumping to conclusions on relational occurrences that are vague can create anxiety in your heart and keep you focused on the wrong things for a very long time. There is an extreme amount of ambiguity in social media. People post and write things online all the time that could be intended in one way, but interpreted in another. Certain things, like sarcasm, for example, are easy to misunderstand.

I have known quiet and reserved people who, for whatever reason, come across as loud and even obnoxious online. Just because someone TYPES EVERYTHING IN ALL CAPS WITH SEVEN EXCLAMATION POINTS AT THE END OF EVERY SENTENCE DOESN'T MEAN THIS PERSON IS BOISTEROUS IN REAL LIFE!!!!!!! LOL!!

Assuming a guy means something when he doesn't state it explicitly is an incorrect assumption and could end up hurting you. Be careful how you interpret.

Second, constantly posting pictures of yourself (selfies) doesn't yield the results you might be looking for. Let me explain. When a woman is in the habit of posting selfies on a regular basis, in a variety of poses, my first thought as a guy isn't, *Wow, she really has a lot of confidence in herself and I'm glad she's sharing what she looks like today because it's totally different from yesterday!* No, I'm actually thinking something along the lines of, *she must crave attention, she seems insecure.*

I know, I know. We're all our own biggest fans. Former NFL player/ personality Terrell Owens was once quoted as saying, "I love me some me." And though many scoffed at his statement when it was made, we're all exactly the same. We love ourselves so much that it's natural to put ourselves on display when we can. It makes sense that we want to post pictures of ourselves online, especially when we like the shots we've taken. They make us look good. However, when you post picture after picture of yourself, it can start to look narcissistic instead of cute. And if any of those photos you post happen to capture a plunging neckline or cleavage, men will be gawking at your pictures for all the wrong reasons. Shots like that usually garner eye rolls and spark the attention of the wrong kind of guy with a wrong set of motives.

Proverbs 11:22 talks about this in a humorous way:

Like a gold ring in a pig's snout is a beautiful woman who shows no discretion.

As Christians, our lives are to be a reflection of Jesus Christ. Are we going to mess up? Yes, of course. But we have to remember that when we post things online, it is an intentional statement and not easily erasable. Once it's out there, it's out there, and there is no taking it back. Seriously consider what you post before you post it, and if there's even the smallest twinge of doubt, don't do it. Godly men love it when godly women make godly choices.

THE DIGITAL CONNECTION

I hope you understand my reasons for mentioning a few of these things. My heart isn't to scold you, but to help set you up for success. When it comes to social media and dating relationships, what used to be a bit of a joke because of its rarity is now commonplace and a regular part of any couple's day-to-day interaction. We have a responsibility to live above reproach and with integrity as followers of Christ. The pitfalls can be plentiful and even alluring when it comes to technology. And although the temptations can be slightly different for men and women, recognizing them is the first step in avoiding the negative effects they can have in our relationships with the opposite sex.

What was true thousands of years ago is still true today—humans crave connection. We live in a profoundly connected world, and we need to use technology well, instead of allowing it to use us.

If you truly want to know a person, spend quality time with him or her. If you only know someone within the context of cyberspace, there's a real possibility that you know this person far less than you think you do. Case in point: the online idiom, *catfish*.

A catfish is someone who pretends to be someone he or she is not, using social media to create a false identity and pursue deceptive online romances (see *Urban Dictionary*)[16]. When people are *catfished*, they are tricked into believing they are connecting with someone online who really isn't the person they thought they were communicating with. There is no substitute for physical talking, walking, and *being* with someone.

One caveat, perhaps, would be online video chatting. You are viewing the face of the other person—albeit across cyberspace—but you are able to comprehend how he or she is responding to you when you talk. Of course face-to-face is preferable, but video chatting is an acceptable substitution when spending time together in the same room isn't possible.

THIS IS EDITED CONTENT

If you want to know me, you need to spend time with me. You can sort-of get to know me if you read about me in my online profiles, but honestly, my profiles are all stuff that I've carefully crafted to portray a polished image of myself. I don't ever post a picture of myself that I don't like. I don't ever type something out on social media that I think will make me sound stupid. Everything I'm putting out there is an edited version of my true self, so a strong argument could be made that online Shelby isn't really Shelby at all. It's a refined and dressed-up Shelby without the flaws.

But if you were to spend any significant amount of time with me, you'd quickly discover that I am extremely flawed. The online version of me doesn't always reflect my true nature because I'm actually *not* perfect, even though my public profile might argue otherwise.

And guess what? Neither are you.

If we know a person solely via the veneer of social media profiles and edited text messages, we don't know that person entirely. Sure, we can begin to understand who a person is by reading what he appreciates, what bands he listens to, what kind of entertainment he enjoys, and what restaurant he'd like to eat at this weekend, but that is only part of the picture. We're deceiving ourselves if we buy into the fact that we can get to know someone deeply or romantically if we only communicate via social media. Typing someone's name into a search engine might partially fulfill your curiosity about the guy or girl you've been thinking about, but you were created for something much deeper than that.

The real you is the real you, and you shouldn't want the person you date to only experience the polished version of your real self. When things progress the way God created them to in the human relational experience, your dating partner will eventually see through the shine of your edited self. I remember a moment from my dating experience with Rachael when I felt the layers peel back, revealing more of the real me than anyone had ever seen before. It was terrifying and wonderful all at the same time. I was tempted to withdraw for fear that she wouldn't like what she saw, but instead I moved toward vulnerability with her, and our relationship only got better. She began to see a more complete picture of who I was, and it made the connection between us more authentic.

This type of genuine relationship cannot happen to the degree you long for via digital media. It will always lack depth because it can never be a substitute for the real thing. A good friend and coworker of mine, Keri Armentrout, puts it this way:

Social media should never be a substitute for relationships, but a springboard for relationships.

I love this. When we harness the potential of social media and employ it as a springboard for something deeper, God can use it for many great things.

SHELBY'S TOP TEN TECHNOLOGICAL NO-NO'S

Which brings us to Shelby's top ten list of things to avoid while blending technology with relationships (both dating and non-dating). You're allowed to disagree, of course, but take the time to consider my reasoning.

1. *Don't ever break up with someone on social media.* I read an article online that talked about the worst ways to break up with someone, and it mentioned a guy who posted a side-by-side picture of himself with his girlfriend on the left, and the same picture with his girlfriend cropped out on the right. He then added the hashtag "#TransformationTuesday." I'm positive every reader of the piece uttered a collective, "What a jerk." Have the guts to talk to the person face-to-face, and don't succumb to the temptation of allowing the digital world to do your dirty work. It's mean. It's immature. It's ungodly. More on this in the chapter on breaking up.

2. *Don't share every detail of your dating relationship online.* We

all know how excited you are to be dating someone, and we're happy for you, but that doesn't mean you need to share every element of every date (complete with pictures) with everyone on social media. Doing this can make others feel annoyed by your constant posting, it can make them frustrated by the fact that they aren't dating anyone, and it can come across as gloating.

Nearly everyone is uncomfortable with public displays of affection, and this is the digital equivalent of that. If you want to post about your relationship, do so sparingly. We'll all be happy you did, and you won't be embarrassed by what you posted when/if you break up.

3. *Don't communicate important things over text messaging.* I read a funny text message conversation between a father and daughter that was posted online, and it helps to illustrate my point.

> Father: *Your mom and I are going to divorce next month.*
> Daughter: *What?! Why? Call me please!*
> Father: *I wrote "Disney" and this phone auto-corrected it. We are going to Disney.*

It is so very easy to be misunderstood in a text message. The tone/mood of what you're trying to say in your head can be quite different from what you actually type out to another person. Or the phone can auto-correct what you type out (as we've just seen). If you have something important to communicate to someone, please don't type it out with your thumbs on a phone. Have the decency to call, or better yet, communicate face-to-face. You wouldn't want to hear that your car blew up via a text because you'd inevitably have a few follow-up questions. Relationships are much more complex and important than a car, so don't utilize a text message when communicating things of significance.

4. *Don't constantly be on your phone when you're with other people.* Another way of putting this is by saying, "Be present." I'm preaching to myself here, but this is a prevalent issue among young people today. If you are talking to someone, and you intentionally pull out your phone to look at something else in the middle of your conversation, you are essentially communicating to the person you're with that he or she isn't as important.

This is something I've been quite convicted about because I do this all the time. If my daughter and I are playing, and I pull out my phone, I'm telling her that whatever is on my phone is more important than my time spent with her. She will eventually pick up on this social norm and follow suit one day. If I continually break away to check my phone, telling her that time spent with her is important won't matter because what I do will always speak louder than what I say...and the same goes for you, too. You can look at the people closest to you and say that you value time with them, but if all you do is spend time "away" from them on your phone while you are together, your actions will say the opposite. It's rude, disrespectful, and devaluing of the person who's right in front of you. Shelby, are you listening to this?

5. *If you're a couple, don't fight on social media.* Arguments, like public displays of affection, are uncomfortable to be around. And when you take to social media to argue with your significant other, it makes others feel extremely awkward. Your fights are your business and not the world's. Keep them where they belong—between the two of you, and offline.

6. *If you're not a couple, don't fight on social media.* Arguments that happen online are pointless. POINTLESS. So many people take to social media or comment sections to yell at others for whatever reason, and nobody listens to anyone. Comment sections online are generally the real-world equivalent to bathroom stall graffiti—angry, mean-spirited, and frothing diatribes that no one should ever read.

   No good has ever come from constant bickering about important issues within the venue of comment posting. Nobody's mind is going to be changed by what you type in an angry post on someone's internet page, so simply don't do it. If you want to inspire real change in another person, don't try to win an argument from the safety of your phone or computer. Show love and care online and in person. If you have an issue with a person, deal with it in the flesh where it isn't safe and you can be held accountable for your words. This is what must happen if we are to represent Jesus in the digital world.

7. *Don't talk to the faceless social media community about your relationship problems.* Similar to arguing online, don't air your grievances about relationship (or lack of relationship) issues for the whole world to see. If you need to talk about your

problems, meet with a friend over coffee, not your keyboard over the internet. When you rant about how "girls suck" or how "guys are such jerks," you end up being very divisive, making others upset with you who don't need to be upset with you. Additionally, your rants can look like a plea for attention. Talk to a sibling, talk to a friend, talk to a counselor...but don't post it online.

8. *Don't get your significance from social media.* As with many other things in this world, social media can quickly become a means by which we gain a sense of significance. I'll admit that I have fallen victim to disappointment if my posts don't get "liked" or "favorited" or "reposted." And when I catch myself feeling that way, I immediately know that my heart needs to be realigned toward God. People's opinion of what I post should never be the barometer by which I gauge how well I'm doing. If they are, I know I have shoved God out of His rightful place of prominence in my life and the opinions of others have become an idol. If my perspective isn't correct, I will begin to worship the "like" or the "repost" instead of my Creator.

It might seem silly to say, but the truth is, it happens all the time. Be very careful about where you gain your significance. If it's in anything other than our Lord and Savior, it will enslave you and mistreat you, leaving you begging for more of its acceptance.

9. *Don't stalk people online—it's creepy.* If you want to get to know someone, you can use social media as a springboard for relationship (like my friend Keri Armentrout said), but

not as a substitute. If you genuinely want to learn about who this person is, spend time with him or her, don't just read about the person online. With the natural normalization of online profiles, everything is becoming more voyeuristic, but if that's all you are doing to gain knowledge about another person, you're missing out on the best part of that person— the *actual* person.

10. *Don't allow texting and social media to diminish your social skills.* If you don't spend time communicating with people, you'll never learn how to communicate with people. Profound, huh? If you never use a muscle, it becomes atrophied and withered. It's wasted space in your body until you begin to use it again and make it bigger and stronger. And the same goes for communication skills.

When all you do is communicate via texting or social media (an edited form of yourself and your communication), you become socially impaired. You don't learn about give-and-take within a conversation. You don't know how to look someone in the eye when you speak or how to be attentive when spoken to. You won't comprehend appropriate social cues on what should or shouldn't be said at the proper moment, and interaction with others will be awkward on a continual basis.

Learning these kinds of things is a skill that must be practiced in real-world scenarios, and this cannot be done behind a screen of any kind. And knowing these skills will make you a more valuable instrument in the hands of our Creator, breeding effective ministry for His glory anywhere you might go. You will also hone the ability to develop poignant and long-lasting relationships with many others.

I'm not saying to stop texting or using social media. Just don't allow the use of texting and social media to shrivel your social capabilities, making your impact for Him weakened, and your relationships wanting.

WOULD YOU GO OUT WITH ME?

Other than on social media, I don't really keep up with many friends from high school. But if you asked anyone who knew me back then if I would be likely to publish a book on dating, they would no doubt pee their pants from laughing so hard. Why? Because I literally dated one girl in high school...and that "relationship" lasted for all of two weeks.

However, when I graduated from high school and went to college, I decided I should probably make up for lost time. I dated a lot of girls in college. Too many girls. And looking back, I now realize that I probably did this because girls finally took an interest in me, and it simply felt good to have the kind of attention and affection I craved all those years in high school. In college, I soaked up every drop of life those romantic feelings gave me, and I went from one girl to the next to the next.

I've already shared with you my personal history of physical intimacy, so you know that those relationships weren't based in the sexual arena, but the truth is that I used women (and the jolt of emotions women provided) to make me feel cared for and important. I may not have used them physically, but it certainly doesn't change the fact that my heart wasn't in the right place when it came to asking a girl out. I didn't do it to serve them...I did it to serve myself.

However, with time and increasing maturity, my perspective regarding my sisters-in-Christ developed nicely and I'm more proud of my actions in the dating realm during the last half of my college career. My number of dates diminished significantly, and at a certain point, I even felt confident enough to speak into the lives of other people on the subject. In fact, during my senior year, I was asked to speak about dating from a Christian perspective on a panel of fraternity and sorority students. Was I in a frat? No, but they also wanted someone on the panel who wasn't greek, so my guess is that I was the proverbial death-of-two-birds-with-one-stone by being a non-greek, Christian student.

I remember vividly what I was feeling as I sat with the other greek students behind a table on that stage: fear. There were around 600 fraternity and sorority students in the audience that night, and I was so absolutely terrified I was going to blow it for all of Christendom by giving a wrong answer or saying something stupid.

Truthfully, though, it ended up being a lot of fun, and I even warmed up the crowd a bit when I made everyone laugh by pointing out a few Christian stereotypes. So when the time came for me to answer a pointed question about what my ideal first date was, I had some credibility in the eyes of the audience when I spoke.

I talked about how the typical first date is often dinner and a movie (at least it was when I was in college), and I went out on a limb to say that I thought a movie is actually a bad first date. "Why would I want to sit next to a girl for two hours, staring at a screen, when I can easily come up with a better idea of how to spend our time?" I said, "Women deserve to be pursued, and going to a movie on a first date doesn't communicate pursuit. I'd rather interact with her and get to know her."

I went on to say that I didn't think going to a movie was a bad date, just a bad *first* date. Then the student president of the inter-fraternity counsel (also on the panel) publicly disagreed with me and this started a fiery debate about what constituted a good first date. This led the discussion into many different directions, including defining the term "hooking up." But I digress. All in all, it was a great time.

As I reflect on that moment from my college life, I still hold the same opinion. When you are getting to know someone, it's important to spend time doing stuff that actually helps you get to know the other person. The argument of the inter-fraternity counsel president that night on the panel was that you can discuss the movie with your date after the film and this would help you get to know one another. In my mind, however, that's a bit of a stretch.

After watching a movie with your date, can you talk and learn more about the heart of the person you just sat next to? Sure...a little. But in reality, there's a much better chance of you discovering more about the other person while conversing over a meal, a walk, a game, or an activity. Asking good questions about real life and listening, instead of discussing whether the romanticism or action in the flick you just saw was realistic, is a far better way to get to know him or her. And this is coming from someone who LOVES movies and television! Trust me—save the movie for date number three (I just picked an arbitrary number...it doesn't have to be the third date).

THE FIRST DATE AND BEYOND

As I've grown older, single people have sometimes asked me, "Do you have any advice on what to do for a first date?" I suppose this question comes with the assumption that I'll be able to give an answer loaded with wisdom and creativity, but the truth is that I can really only say what I did on my first date with my wife, and this isn't necessarily what other first dates should look like. Even though the question is uniform, the answer is not. Everyone is different. When I'm asked this question, I usually throw out some personal stories from my past, but then I quickly transition into questions about what they or their date might like.

Take baseball for an example: a minor league ballgame that's close by would make a great first date for any guy or girl who loves the game. There's lots of time to talk and listen in an environment that's interesting.

Maybe a couple is the creative type. A painting class, or pottery lesson, wrapped up with a walk in nature would probably be a hit. Or perhaps two people prefer the chill environment; go to a coffee shop and talk for a while before heading to dinner at a favorite restaurant. The important thing is to put some effort into the date. Find out what the other person might enjoy, and then roll with the punches as you experience trial and error along the way.

I started simple with Rachael. Our first date was actually a group date. A bunch of college guys I was leading in a Bible study asked her Bible study group out on a creative group date (my guys were unaware of my interest in Rachael...honest). As a company of dudes, we surprised the girls at their Bible study. We had re-written the words to Frank Sinatra's *Fly Me to the Moon*, and when we showed up, we sang a cappella, asking them to join us on a date. A few weeks later, we met as a group (about twenty of us). The guys made dinner and dessert, we played a few group games, and we even gave each girl a little gift of encouragement in the form of a glass vase and a flower.

It was a tremendously positive time for everyone involved, and it genuinely helped me get to know Rachael in a smaller public setting. This was important to me because I was very interested to learn what kind of a person she was as she interacted with her friends and other people in a more intimate social setting. I had only had my eye on her for a couple of months, and our interactions had been limited to larger group settings when there were 500-600 people around (kinda hard to get to know someone that way).

Her social interactions with the other girls in her Bible study and my guys made an impression on me, so I became intentional about seeking her out in group settings and chatting about various things in both of our lives. Eventually, I knew I wanted to spend more one-on-one time with her, so I asked her if she'd be willing to get some coffee with me. She agreed, and I picked her up one afternoon and took her to a local coffee shop to explain what I was thinking and feeling. I simply told her that I was interested in her (in case she hadn't noticed), and I wanted to spend more time with her. I suppose you could call our time together at that coffee shop our first date, but we didn't really label it until much later in our relationship.

We didn't label it because we didn't really go out all that much in the coming weeks. We were both busy people and I was intentional about communicating to her that I wanted to spend more time with her, but not necessarily alone. So we hung out together with her roommates, with my roommates, in groups of friends, and in organized social settings. I believe we got to know one another in a genuine way by stepping into one another's lives without detaching ourselves from our own daily lives.

Eventually, we placed the official label of "dating" on our relationship. By doing this, we communicated to one another that we weren't going to date anyone else. We were a couple, but it took some time to get there...a fact about our relationship I'm quite proud of. As a couple, we went out to dinner, hung out, played games, went for walks, visited cool places, went to museums, ice skated, and eventually met each other's families. I created a lot of hand-made stuff for her along the way (including a choose-your-own-adventure date booklet—yeah!), and we did a lot of stuff that kind of flopped in the way of fun, but I put effort into it, and she loved that.

It was wonderful, and it worked for us, but you might hate art museums, or bowling, or even movies. Take time to come up with things that you are both interested in or something only your date is interested in and you would like to learn more about. Pray, and think, and be open to something new. I'm personally thankful for the choices Rachael and I made in the early part of our dating relationship, and I'm glad that I put forethought into our times together. I cared about her and she cared about me, and that was reflected in what we did when we dated. Think through questions, such as

What does my date actually enjoy?

How can I incorporate what my date enjoys into our time together?

What is the best way I can encourage my date when we get together?

These are good questions when we remember that a date is a Divine Appointment To Encourage. Plan and prepare, and be thoughtful of the other person in the process. You can't go wrong with this kind of attitude, even if the date ends up being lame because the restaurant you go to is really bad. When you're intentional about breathing life into the other person (ahem...metaphorically), the first date and subsequent dates will be a delight, regardless of the relationship's outcome.

Additionally, because dating is by nature selective, understand that there is something extremely healthy and godly about a group date. A group date can create an environment in which you can have a nice time with the opposite sex without communicating romantic interest.

A group date allows you to think about a date from the perspective of one who might otherwise be left out or alone. When our Bible study groups got together, one of the best things about it was that it was all-inclusive. It was an opportunity to bring encouragement to a large group of people (a very Christ-like thing), bring health to a body of believers, and bring glory to the name of Jesus.

THE UGLY "TRUTH" ABOUT DATING

I recently read an article online that talked about the eighteen ugly truths concerning modern dating that young people have to deal with, and to say the very least, the piece made me sad. A few things, however, popped out in the article that gave me pause and made me wonder about the truth of these supposed truths.

Near the top of the list was the statement, "Set plans are dead. If you aren't the top priority, your invitation to spend time [together] will be given a 'maybe' or 'I'll let you know,' and the deciding factor(s) will be whether that person has offers more fun/interesting than you on the table."[17]

While this might be true for some people, allow me to point out the glaring lack of respect it holds for any person who might be tangled in its web. If set plans are dead, it's because the people who allowed them to die are lazy or selfish. Fear of missing out (FOMO) is an infectious disease in modern times that can easily be cured by men who care enough to intentionally think ahead about what they want to do on a date, and women who respectfully don't flake out once a date has been planned. Sure, there might be other things that come up when you have a date planned, but being an adult means following through with what you've committed to do with another person regardless of other shiny events that might compete for your attention.

FOMO doesn't exist in most other areas of life. One example of this would be the workplace. If you decide to skip out on a business meeting that has been planned at your office in favor of going to the zoo with your pals from college, you get fired. Why? Because making commitments and following through with those commitments is what mature people do, and there are consequences for those who are unreliable. Why, then, do the rules suddenly change in the dating arena? "Well, because I want to have control over my social life, and if something better comes up at the last minute, I have the right to do that instead," one might say.

I understand this line of thinking...if it were communicated by an eleven-year-old. When you stop and examine the FOMO statement above, you begin to realize how often it's adopted these days and also how incredibly selfish it is. "I want what I want, and I want it when I want it! My respect for other people and their feelings be damned!" is essentially what's being communicated. As followers of Jesus Christ, we are called to live life differently, not become wrapped up in the overwhelming trend of FOMO, leaving other people's feelings and plans trampled.

> ...but let your "yes" be yes and your "no" be no, so that you may not fall under condemnation. (James 5:12b)

When a guy asks a girl out, he is living out his call to initiate with a woman. He should plan the date, think about what she might enjoy on the date, care about her well-being on the date, respect her by showing up on time (even if she's not ready when he gets there to pick her up), think about what he wants to talk about with her on the date, intentionally listen to her answers when he asks questions on the date, focus on encouraging her on the date, and finally, thank her for joining him for their time together.

When a girl agrees to go out with a guy, she is living out her call to respond to a man's initiation. She should expect that the guy has made a plan for their time together. She should feel cared for on the date, encouraged on the date, and respected on the date. If she has agreed to join him, she shouldn't make other plans with anyone else for the entire time they are on the date. She should be *present*, meaning she shouldn't be texting other friends or people. She should listen to her date when he talks and respond to his questions when he shows interest in her life. She should respect him just as he is respecting her, and when their time together is over, she should thank him for the effort he put into the date.

Mutual care, mutual encouragement, and mutual life-giving. Not selfishness, FOMO, or flakiness. These are the qualities that matter. The sad article I mentioned earlier also said, "The person who cares *less* has all the power. Nobody wants to be the one who's more interested." This is not only sad, it's childish.

I understand the tempting appeal this kind of perspective holds when it comes to manipulation and an attempt to have power over another person in the context of a relationship. But a strong argument for abandoning immaturity and moving on to something more fulfilling and godly is the common sentiment that people are sick of the dating scene as it exists. Dating should never be about who has more power in a relationship. Neither should it be about caring less in order to feel better about the amount of control you hold over the person you're interested in. It should be the exact opposite.

One of two things is going to happen in any and every relationship: you're either going to break up, or you're going to get married. This reality should drive the way you go about the beginning and middle stages of your interaction with that person. You simply cannot build a foundation of flakiness, manipulation, or laziness in any relationship and expect it to flourish in a healthy way. Wrestling for this illusion of control will do nothing but harm.

No woman is out there hoping to marry a man who doesn't put

any effort into showing her thoughtfulness and care on a date. "Oh, it was so precious! He texted me and said, 'Wanna hang out sometime?' And after blowing me off for three weeks, we finally got together, watched some stupid movie on his couch, and then he tried to kiss me before we even talked about anything of depth! It was almost like he didn't care about me at all! Magical!" Nope. No woman is praying for that kind of guy.

God calls us to far more than this. Instead of moving backwards into immaturity, progress forward into maturity, godliness, and health. The verse that applies to playing games in relationships applies here as well:

> *When I was a child, I spoke like a child, I thought like a child, I reasoned like a child. When I became a man, I gave up childish ways.* (1 Corinthians 13:11)

I DON'T FEEL CALLED TO YOU
ANYMORE: THE BREAKUP

All the broken hearts in the world still beat.[18]
-Ingrid Michaelson

Christians have this habit of letting God take the blame for their dirty work when it comes to the end of dating relationships. Many Christian women and men have been on the receiving end of the phrase, "I just don't feel called to you anymore," or "I don't think God is calling us to be together." Myself included.

In my mid-twenties, I was dating a girl who essentially said this to me and by doing so nailed the proverbial coffin closed on our relationship. I couldn't help but think to myself after she said it, "But I feel that God is still calling us to be together...so who's not hearing from God correctly?" Apparently, it was me because we didn't date anymore after that conversation.

And as sincere as I believe she was when she broke up with me, it kind-of made me mad that she used The Creator as a scapegoat for what she actually wanted. There were many times in the weeks following our breakup when I wished she would have just told me what she felt straight-up: "I don't like you anymore, and I think we should break up." I know that probably would've stung more, but at least I'd have definitive closure without wondering why each of us was hearing something completely different from God.

As much as we want to spiritualize a breakup, the truth is that God has given us natural sensibilities, feelings, and desires for certain relationships, and when they come to an end (for whatever reason), we need to take responsibility, instead of pointing the finger at God and saying, "Uh...He did it!"

SOFTENING THE BLOW

Sure, when we know that it's time for a dating relationship to come to an end, we want to do everything we can to try to help the broken-up-with person feel like he or she hasn't been mercilessly beaten down. We've been in a romantic relationship with that person, and to some degree, we still care very much about his or her feelings. But there is a difference between gently communicating the way you're feeling about the relationship's inevitable conclusion and incriminating God for the fact that you are ready for it to be over.

Maybe you *are* feeling that the Lord is leading you away from your boyfriend or girlfriend, but remember, communication is an art that must be crafted carefully in all circumstances. You don't want to come across as condescending and make your ex feel like he or she is a fragile child who needs to be pandered to. God may, in fact, be leading you in a different direction, but is that really something your ex needs to hear at this exact moment? Theology lessons in times of extreme emotion often don't fall well on sad or hurt hearts.

I hope you would never walk up to a widow at the funeral of her late husband and say, "You should cheer up because Romans 8:28 says '...*we know that in all things God works for the good of those who love him, who have been called according to his purpose.*'" Why? Because even though it's true (after all, it is Scripture), it can be insensitive when used at an inappropriate time.

When you pull God into the middle of your breakup, even though your intentions are based on compassion for the other person, it can do more harm than good. Don't try to cushion the blow by adding a layer of Jesus to your relationship's demise. Take responsibility for your feelings and communicate with maturity in a way that respects the time you've shared with the other person. As your brother or sister in Christ, this person deserves your forthright consideration.

HAVE THE GUTS TO DO IT RIGHT

The digital age has not only influenced relationships and communication in the modern era, but it has also essentially transformed the way people break up. Here, allow me to refer back to my previous rant regarding the use of social media in dating: breaking up via a text message is cowardly.

This is not middle school, people. Important communication needs to happen face-to-face. Do not begin a relationship with a digital barrier, and likewise, don't end a relationship with a digital barrier. Is it easier to send an email, text, or social media message telling the other person that you want to break up? Of course it's easier! Knowing he's the one who made it happen, no guy wants to see mascara mixed with tears streaming down a girl's face. Knowing she's the reason he's crying for only the third time in his adult life, no girl wants to see a man reduced to a sobbing mess with his hands cupped over his face. Looking at someone when you break up with him or her sucks... but it's the adult thing to do.

You've got to have the guts to look someone in the eyes and tell him or her the truth that you aren't going to be dating anymore. Don't hide behind your computer or phone as a safe conduit for your lack of ambitious communication. Hard times are inevitable, and when you constantly avoid the other person via digital devices, you're robbing yourself of the opportunity to grow into a healthier person who is able to handle the inevitable complications that come with being an adult.

The culture we live in constantly tempts us to extend our adolescence by dangling options in our faces that are immediately comfortable, but when we routinely choose comfort, we sacrifice character. Success without character can lead to dangerous and destructive places which is why many people who experience success early in life end up falling apart when reality eventually smacks them in the face. It's not hard to think of a few famous people who had the limelight forced on them early in their career and later tanked when they hit a few bumps in the road. Difficulty strengthens integrity. A muscle must be broken down before it builds up—this is the way life works.

Breaking up with someone through a text message will not make things easier. In reality, it will make you weaker. It compromises your moral fiber, and it dishonors God. You are Christ's ambassador

(2 Corinthians 5:20), and you represent Him to every other person you come in contact with, including the person you've decided not to date anymore.

TRUST ME, I KNOW FROM EXPERIENCE

I've been broken up with. Multiple times, in fact. And although none of those instances were much fun, they were a necessary part of my story that led me to where I am today. Of course I was really sad when those moments happened, but like (nearly) every other person who's been broken up with, I got over it.

I moved on, and God directed me toward my wife, Rachael. Since I've been with her, I've never once thought, "Man, I wish I were still dating that other girl." That would be crazy. But I'll tell you what—I have often wished that those girls who broke up with me would have ripped the metaphorical Band-Aid off more quickly and more truthfully.

If you're the one doing the dumping, please walk strongly with Jesus and in the power of His Spirit. Be kind and caring and do the deed right. And if you're on the receiving end of the dump (pun intended), please walk strongly with Jesus and in the power of His Spirit when it happens. Take it better than I did.

Experiencing the pain of a breakup is an opportunity to embrace difficult circumstances in which our will, our plan, and our desires are subverted for a better plan—God's. Hearing "no" to our dreams for a certain relationship can sometimes prompt anger and even rebellion, but if we humble ourselves under God's mighty hand when the rug gets pulled out from under our feet, we grow in obedience and humility, like Abraham sacrificing Isaac.

In Genesis 22, Abraham was asked by God to give up his only son as a sacrifice to the Lord. Abraham was willing and obedient to God to the point of lifting the knife above his son's body while believing God would supply another sacrifice. God stopped Abraham in the process and provided a ram for him to sacrifice instead of his son. The point is that Abraham was faithful the entire time and willing to give up something extremely precious to him because God asked him to. No doubt Abraham was scared, confused, and grieved that God was taking away his only son, but he trusted his Creator. He believed that through it all, God knew best.

Leaning in and learning to handle hard situations in a mature way is formative. Much spiritual immaturity can be traced back to an unwillingness to view by faith the things that God allows and does not allow in our lives. It's important to be okay with God when He's not cooperating with *our* plans. It takes practice to humbly accept the answer "no" and to understand that this answer (though we may not want to hear it) is rooted in God's deep love and providence for our lives.

Remember, even if you break up, you're both still siblings in Christ, and this really does mean something. Though you may not fully understand why things are happening the way they are, Jesus still rules over every detail.

In his heart a man plans his course, but the Lord determines his steps. (Proverbs 16:9)

LESS HUNTING, MORE GROWTH

Many conversations and debates take place among Christians regarding whether or not God has that one perfect person for everyone. There are varying opinions, of course, and the topic is probably on the mind of nearly every single Christian person on the planet. *Is there someone out there for me? Is it my responsibility to take the wheel from Jesus and find my soul mate?*

Good thoughts. Important thoughts. And extremely relevant to a generation of singles who wonder how involved they should be in the process of finding a mate. Personally, I thought I had the answer figured out when I was a college student. Not necessarily because of my own personal experience in the dating world (which you now know was less than stellar), but because of how I viewed the young men I respected as they traveled the relationship road ahead of me.

As an underclassman, I watched many godly men date, get engaged, get married, and start a family. I rejoiced with them, and I took mental notes on how I needed to emulate the good practices they set forth in their relationships. Time marched on, and I approached the end of college. I saw many close friends find "the one" for them and get married to women who loved Jesus and wanted to glorify Him in their lives. It was great, and what I witnessed only reinforced my understanding that there is a perfect person for everyone who loves and genuinely follows Christ.

But then something happened. A very close friend whom I admired and respected spiritually told me one evening that he was thinking of getting a divorce. He explained that things with his wife of a few years weren't going well and had, in fact, been bad for a while. Even though they tried to work on it by having a baby to "fix" their problems (yep, he was also a new father), they just couldn't seem to make it work, and they were probably going to split very soon.

I was floored. I literally couldn't believe it when he first told me. I thought he was kidding. I didn't understand how this could be true. Both my friend and his wife were solid followers of Jesus. They had both been on missionary trips overseas, led Bible studies, discipled younger believers, led worship, and served as the faces of leadership within our college ministry. My friend had found "the one" we always believed was out there for him. How could the formula be broken?

Sadly, my friend did get divorced. His ex-wife got remarried, and to this day my friend is still single. Of course, when his marriage first started, he and his wife made some choices that led to the crumbling of their young relationship, but needless to say, this whole story complicated my mindset. Was there really only one person, chosen by God, just for me? Truthfully, it made me a lot more nervous about something that felt much easier when I believed I would eventually find the person I was destined to spend my life with. And like any belief system, it began to shape my day-to-day actions.

Dating relationships for me weren't fun experiences I enjoyed anymore. They took on more of a frantic, hunting-for-the-right-person vibe. I became a bit obsessed with trying to discover this "right person." In fact, even when I liked a certain girl, my thoughts could haunt me: *Is she the right one?* I began to place girls I dated under a microscope of scrutiny that no person could ever feasibly live up to. I evaluated every little thing about the way they spoke, the way they ate, their study habits, their families, and their dating histories. Why does she dress the way she does? What does it say about her that her best friend is weird? Does her hair pile up in the sink too much when she brushes it? Does she like to sleep in on the weekends the way I do? I wonder if she likes the same kind of movies and music I do? It was varied, irrational, and, well, ridiculous.

But (by the grace of God!) a moment came when I realized I should probably spend a lot less energy finding the right person and more on becoming the right person. I found that when most of my attention was focused on the girl, I was neglecting some great opportunities to allow the Lord to develop me. I was worried about how sanctified my date was when I should have been concentrating on God's sanctifying work in my life. Perhaps this is obvious in light of the previous paragraph, but for whatever reason, I needed a brief hiatus into my own personal Shelby-orbit before I figured out that I, myself, was a big problem who required significant work. What a jerk I was, huh?

Ah, but our God is a forgiving God, and as I gave this area over to Him, He helped me to see that defect in my life. I asked for forgiveness and have since tried to allow Jesus to influence my opinions of others and see them through His eyes, not my judgmental ones. It has been a process, but God changed me from within because all things are possible with Him (Mark 10:27).

THE LIST

My guess is that you probably have some sort of list you keep, either physical or mental, that helps you determine if the man or woman you're interested in might be your future spouse. It's a common practice for a lot of people in the single world. In fact, a friend of mine once showed me her "Ideal Man" list she kept in her Bible, of all places. It had bullet points, such as "must play the guitar," and, "needs to have a good relationship with his parents." When she showed it to me, I remember reading through her list and quietly laughing at its absurdity. What if she met a guy who was an orphan and didn't have parents? What if he played the drums and not the guitar? Would that still count? What if he played no instrument at all? *Ridiculous*, I thought. But not too long after I saw my friend's list, I had to acknowledge that I kept a mental list of my own. Perhaps my list wasn't quite as specific as hers, but I still had one. Who's the ridiculous one now, Shelby?

Of course, as God would have it, I ended up marrying a wonderful girl who failed to meet some of the "most important" criteria on my mental index of requirements. When I held tightly to the qualities I thought the future Mrs. Abbott should possess, I sincerely believed that she should:

- Share my love for television, movies, and pop culture.
- Enjoy sleeping in whenever possible because she is a night person like me.
- Have a vast knowledge of the music world so we can always converse about the latest tune that moves us in a way that cuts straight to the heart.

These things were crucial to me at the time, and I didn't think it was too much to expect God to connect me with a woman who checked off the boxes. Reality, however, aligned me with Rachael (and by 'reality,' I mean 'God'). Rachael simply didn't care about TV shows. If she went the rest of her life without watching anything on television, she'd be just fine. Movies? She could take them or leave them. And when it comes to pop culture, I usually end up explaining to her what is happening in that world.

Rachael is also a morning person. If she had her choice, she'd go to bed every night at around 10:00 pm and wake up at 6:00 am to start her day. She likes music (nearly every human being likes music), but she honestly doesn't care about cool new bands or discovering new artists in the music medium the way that I do. On paper, Rachael wouldn't have been the right choice for me at all. And Rachael, I might add, firmly believed she would marry a man who is tall. She had only seriously dated guys who were over six feet tall, and Rachael was convinced she'd end up with a towering man. Enter into the picture, me: a five foot, six inch modern-day hobbit who swept her off her feet. God has a wonderful sense of humor. But now—thank you Jesus—Rachael is my all-time best friend in the entire world, and I absolutely love spending any time with her that I can.

Oh, and in case you were wondering, we aren't an "opposites attract" kind of couple. We share a lot in common in the way of personality, spirituality, life philosophy, humor, and communication style. All told, we have nearly everything in common with what we want our lives to look like except for those three things I listed earlier. What I once thought was absolutely necessary in a life partner became obsolete when I understood that God had called me to marry Rachael. It's absolutely okay that she doesn't like some of the recreational activities I do, and it's okay (most of the time) that she's a morning person. She's the perfect mate for me, and I'm thankful that God brought us together despite what I thought I "knew" was my perfect girl.

Of course, my point in sharing this with you is to help you see that what we believe needs to be fundamentally true about the person we're looking for isn't always what the Lord leads us to. We spend so much time looking around and weeding out certain types of people because they don't fit in a specific category when in reality we should be focusing on our own relationship with God and trusting Him to bring along the right person in our lives at the right time. We need to hunt around less and spiritually grow more.

If the dating pool were full of men and women who cared more about walking with Jesus and less about who we should be partnering up with, I believe the body of Christ would be substantially more transformative in God's Kingdom. Our selfish mistakes would dwindle in light of a more healthy desire to bring day-to-day glory to Christ. As human beings, we tend to look on the outside while our Creator would have us look inward. When the root is deep, the fruit is produced. Finding the right person isn't necessarily the goal. Being the right person, however, is.

THE ONLINE DATING VARIABLE

An added wrinkle to this whole conversation comes with the onset of internet dating. This is a variable that simply didn't exist for much of the time when I was single. We are just beginning to understand how this can be done in a healthy way and how the Lord can work in the process. It brings into question the balance between our diligence and God's sovereignty in a rather important way, similar to the way birth control did when it arrived on the scene.

How much responsibility do we have in this dating world, and how much responsibility belongs to God? Birth control brought this issue to the forefront by offering people control over when/if they wanted to conceive children. Many followers of Christ were (and still are) very much against it, and another large section of the Christian community embraces it.

Similarly (in principle), online dating opens up a world of possibilities that weren't an option before the internet. It used to be that if you didn't meet a spouse in your natural circle of friends and family, you might begin to think that perhaps the Lord was calling you to a life of singleness. Now, however, if the tiny pond you're fishing in hasn't yielded any nibbles on the line, you can simply start fishing in the vast dot-com ocean. Can this be a good thing? Sure! Online dating has been responsible for a lot of great and godly marriages.

But while it provides a variety of options, with great power comes great responsibility. As with any good thing, an added tension drifts onto the scene when we have the opportunity to take matters into our own hands—it becomes easy to lose sight of God's plan for our lives. Yes, there are so many wonderful things about online dating and the possibility of finding the love of your life, but we must be careful to hold that power with revered faithfulness toward Jesus. It's possible He wants you to connect with someone online, start dating, get engaged, get married, have 3.7 kids, and buy a dog...but He might also want you to be single. Just because you *can* take matters into your own hands doesn't necessarily mean that you *should* take matters into your own hands.

If things aren't moving quickly enough for you, be careful not to enter into a state of relationship panic and sign up for SingleMingle. com or HisPerfectSpouseForMeRightNow.com (those aren't real websites). Singleness is an opportunity to prayerfully consider what the Lord might have for you if you decide to engage with an online dating profile. Take your desires to the Lord and ask Him for direction and clarity in what to pursue and not pursue when dating via technology. Don't do it simply because your personal connections with the people around you in your own pond have floundered (pun intended). Do it because you believe God is intentionally calling you to broaden your search by dating online. This is food for thought as we wrestle with the complexities of singleness in the technological age.

ANSWER THE QUESTION!

So, after covering all of this, we still haven't answered the question, "Is there a perfect person for everyone?" As I mentioned earlier,

I used to think so, but after having a front row seat to a few derailing pieces of evidence that point to the contrary (like my good friend who got divorced), I'd have to say now that I don't know. Maybe it's more of a theological question with extremely educated and godly people on both sides of the argument. I'm not sure.

What I will say, however, is that I can't imagine another person in the world more perfect for me than my wife. I believe God brought us together in His flawless timing and that makes me limitlessly thankful for a gift I didn't deserve. Yes, I was intentional about pursuing her, but at the same time, I was faithfully trusting the Lord in the process of my pursuit.

It's like the Christian saying that goes, "Work as if it all depends on you, and pray as if it all depends on God." I like that. It marries the idea of our involvement and God's sovereignty quite nicely, even with the inclusion of the online dating variable. How does a paradox like that work? I have no idea, but I see many places in Scripture that describe the all-knowing, all-powerful God, and at the same time I see the Lord's call in our lives to take action and live on mission in a way that brings glory and honor to His name. It's less of an either/or, and more of a both/and scenario, and we are wise to apply it to every area of our lives, including the realm of dating.

THE "IT" FACTOR

I have a lot of friends and family who have gone to dating websites and tested the digital waters. I've heard a lot of stories that ended in failure (some very funny), and I know of others that led to marriage. The online dating world is a mixed bag, but the universal thing seems to be that reading about someone on a website can only get you so far.

Again, building a profile online is great...but it's also edited. If you want to get to know someone, meet and spend time with him or her face-to-face. A digital dating profile is like a resumé. Everyone is going to put their best self out there (as it should be), but when you're looking for a perfect match, you need to keep this in mind. There will inevitably be hidden layers with everyone. Multiple matches can be suggested from computer programming because there may be a lot of people who seem perfect for you on paper, but meeting someone in person is the only true way to find out if there is a connection worth deeper pursuit.

A good friend of mine tried a dating website for a few years. She was matched with three different guys over the course of a few months and in the end, she said, "Some of these guys seemed absolutely perfect when I read about them and even interacted with them online. But when we met face-to-face, I just knew that the 'it' factor wasn't there."

Even though some of the matches seemed exciting, they turned out to be not the right thing for her. In fact, even though the site continued to couple my friend with a lot of guys, she eventually ended up taking her profile down because that avenue of dating simply didn't work for her. She never made the right connection with a guy who she believed had the "it" factor.

And when she mentioned that term, "it" factor, I knew exactly what she was talking about. When someone tries to set a friend up on a blind date with another person they think would be a great match, the reasoning behind the setup is often because of the preconceived idea that they'd hit it off and make a good connection. Matchmaker hearts are usually very much in the right place. However, blind dates often don't work out because the connection has begun without the initial social testing for the "it" factor.

Even though you may call it something different, or have no label for it whatsoever, you probably know what I mean when I refer to the "it" factor. Is it sexual attraction? Is it commonality? Is the absence of "it" simply boredom? Not necessarily. The "it" factor is that inexplicable spark two people feel for one another even after every other factor about their compatibility is laid aside.

Boy meets girl, and though they have nothing in common, they're still attracted to one another for no logical reason other than, "I like her,"...and "I like him." Or, girl discovers boy's interests, observes him in his natural habitat for a period of time, realizes that they have a lot in common, and the "it" factor takes shape. It's not just physical attraction; anything could be responsible for the "it" factor coming to life, and there's really no formula for how it's supposed to play out. In fact, to try and map the genesis of the "it" factor would probably negate it altogether. Sometimes it simply doesn't make sense—it just is what it is.

So where does that leave us if the "it" factor can't be defined? Logic would say that trying to force the "it" factor won't work if it doesn't exist in the relationship in the first place or if it happens to fade in an already existing relationship. Earlier, I talked to you about how a few girls broke up with me because they simply didn't like me anymore. The "it" factor went away for them, and no matter what I did, I couldn't magically make it reappear. They just knew it was over, even if I didn't realize it was over. I tried to figure out the reasons, but even when there seemed to be reasonable answers for why they didn't like me, the majority of the time I found myself confused and hurt, asking, "I'm a good guy, right? I love the Lord and I treated her well...so why doesn't she want to be with me?"

Looking back, I was probably asking the wrong questions. The "it" factor was there, and then it wasn't. Simple as that.

Relationships begin and end all the time. Sometimes they form because the illusion of the "it" factor is there, and they inevitably die when the illusion fades. Sometimes a couple tries to force the "it" factor because they seem to be perfect for one another, but they just don't feel the spark even though all the boxes are checked on their list of requirements in a dating partner. And sometimes the "it" factor ignites a relationship into existence, developing it into serious dating, engagement, then marriage. It's tough to tell how the whole thing works.

That being said, I think it's significant to give credence to the "it" factor instead of making the mistake of dismissing it altogether. It is a real thing. It may not be easy to nail down in any given relationship because it's not a universal quality, but it's certainly real.

And while it is a real thing, it's not the *only* thing. A lot of couples break up solely because they believe the "it" factor isn't there for them, when in truth, they've mistakenly labeled the "it" factor as sexual attraction. If someone makes a decision to end a relationship based solely on the lack of a sexual spark, they're being foolish. Physical attraction in a relationship is an idol that too many people in our culture worship, so starting to build on top of that quality alone will lead you to disappointment.

Charm is deceptive, and beauty is fleeting. (Proverbs 31:30a)

Many factors about relationships, romance, and dating remain a mystery despite our best efforts to give definition to them, but we need to be okay with this. Why? Because when you are in the Kingdom of God, it's important to be fine with the fact that we have the Creator of the universe in our corner, sovereignly guiding those who are faithful to listen to His directional voice.

If the "it" factor wasn't enough to make your last relationship bloom into something permanent, then continue to walk with God and trust Him enough to believe that He knows what's better for you. As much as it hurt when I got broken up with, I praise God that it happened because if I were still with any one of those girls, I wouldn't be with Rachael. I know that sounds a bit like a country song, but it's true. I'm so glad those women ended our dating relationships. I certainly couldn't see that, nor did I have the right kind of perspective when everything in my life hurt because of the breakup. But without the end of those relationships, I wouldn't have my wife.

God is the perfect wedding planner, so let Him pick the most important element of your wedding—your spouse. And *if* (remember: singleness is a good thing) the moment comes for you to wed the one God has chosen for you, I promise you won't be thinking about how much it hurt when some random breakup happened in your history because the "it" factor vanished.

WHAT WOMEN/MEN WANT

What do women want in a man? What qualities are men looking for in a woman? These questions are often raised in movies, television, internet articles, and even blanket books that provide lists on the thirty-eight things every woman should do to land herself a man, or the top ten things a Christian woman is looking for in a godly man. However, addressing these questions formulaically can be dangerous. Often, the cases that become exceptions to the rules pile up higher than those that fall under the "normal" categories explained in detail inside an article or book. There's no such thing as normal because everyone's different.

What might seem super appealing to one person can fall flat with another. For example, I could tell you that girls like guys who are athletic and work out multiple times a week. Now, that might be true for a lot of girls, but there are just as many women out there who are repulsed by the idea that a man can spend a considerable amount of time at a gym all week, every week. Opinions and tastes vary.

Comic books, tattoos, music, camping, photography, video games, poetry, theater, role playing games, dancing, motorcycles, hipster eyeglasses, cosplay...people are in to what they are in to. There is no universal answer to the question, "What do women/men want?"

As Christians, however, we can begin to narrow the playing field a bit in a few specific ways. We should be looking for a Christian mate, of course. If someone's not a Christian, he or she shouldn't be an option. After that, however, many personal preferences get thrown into the mix, and the road splinters in a million different directions.

Rule one though, as far as I'm concerned: Your mate should be a big fan of you, and a bigger fan of Jesus. It's important not to fall into the trap of trying to become someone you aren't in order to make another person happy. This is a charade that can only last for a small amount of time. I've often heard celebrities give advice in various interviews, and time and time again, they come back to the phrase, "Just be yourself." And as cliché as it might sound when they try to project depth as they plug whatever entertainment piece they're promoting, those celebrities are right. You simply have to be you when you swim around in the dating pool.

My grandma used to say, "If you won't be you, who will be?" So until we find a way to start cloning humans, the answer will remain the same: nobody. If the person you like doesn't like you for any reason, those reasons probably aren't going change unless the Lord Himself changes them. Molding yourself into someone you think the other person wants you to be is a mistake that can waste serious amounts of time and cause a lot of heartache. Don't do it.

Love Jesus and be you. That will be exactly what someone out there will want. And as you walk with God, He will lead you to the right person in the appropriate time.

Whether we like it or not, the culture we live in feeds off of stereotypes. Our culture implies that if we only change certain things about ourselves (our hair, our clothes, our hobbies, our car, our everyday activities, etc.), the entirety of the opposite sex will come flocking to our door in no time.

"Lose fifteen pounds and grow your hair out, and the guys will come running."

"Put on fifteen pounds of muscle and learn how to longboard around town, and every girl will want to date you."

And sure, you might laugh at fictional examples like these, but the Christian culture has been duped into believing them as well. I ended up doing and saying a lot of things I didn't want to do or say when I was single because I thought that was what everyone else in my Christian subculture was doing, and I wanted to catch myself a girlfriend.

But there isn't a universal list of qualities that women want in a godly man. There isn't a complete catalogue of specifics you can flip through in order to become the perfect Christian woman who every guy wants to date. As much as we like to have things narrowed down and placed next to neat little boxes that we are able to check off as we look for our perfect person, life is not that simple. Yes, certain qualities should be deal breakers (i.e. don't marry a person who believes he can time-travel back to 1864 and have conversations with Abraham Lincoln), but there are many variables, and this makes it impossible to give general answers to specific questions.

What do women want? What do men want? A lot of things, but we aren't searching for what a television show, or a magazine, or a commercial is telling us to desire. We're believing that if God is calling us to be in a relationship, He will lead us to the right person whom He has set aside for us. And if you are called to be in a relationship, and someone you like comes into your life, you won't care what everyone else wants because you'll be content with what the Lord has blessed you with. Nobody else's opinion of who you should be will matter.

KEEP THE MAIN THING THE MAIN THING

The "it" factor was something I wrestled with throughout my single years, especially when I was going through the heartache of a breakup. I'm able to understand it a bit more now because I'm on the far end of those relationships looking back with a refined sense of clarity I didn't possess when I was in the moment. Hurt, frustration, insecurity, and hormones can add a lot of haze to decision making when you're single, so it's extremely important to dwell on the truth of who God is when everything else about your relationship status is in chaos.

You will make mistakes, and some of those mistakes might cause a lot of pain for the guy or girl you're in a relationship with, but cutting through the confusion to get to clarity regarding God's direction in your life can save you and your significant other tons of unnecessary grief.

Keep the main thing the main thing. Sometimes "why?" is simply the wrong question to ask when you're in the middle of relationship woes. If the "it" factor isn't there, consider it a good thing. Stop speculating. Your love life is not in the toilet, and God has something better because He loves you so crazy much!

Dwelling on this reality will yield the contentment, maturity, and peace you truly long for. When you live here, you reside in the sweet spot every Christian is designed for—a life of faith.

CONCLUSION

At the beginning of this book, I used a metaphor with which I attempted to explain the finer intricacies of dating. I likened it to a dance. I said that dealing well with the opposite sex isn't a science because it's not static, or predictable, or easy, or analytical. You might even step on a few toes because it can be awkward and messy when the music begins.

The universal appeal of dating makes it a subject worthy to be tackled by godly men and women who desire to exalt Jesus in an area where few people know how. I have provided you with some of the practical do's and don'ts of dating and relationships, but life itself is a much better teacher than research. In the end, you're going to have to just feel the music and go for it on your own.

As someone who has spent a significant amount of time around single people, I have witnessed a lot of painful relationships that have prevented many young people from fully focusing on what the Lord wants in their lives. I've witnessed (and personally experienced) much defeat, and it has been prevalent and unpleasant. In light of this, and God's work in my own life, I felt led to write something that would provide clarity to friendships, maturity, communication, mutual respect, and grounding in the Lord Jesus Christ. I wanted to create a tool that would have been helpful to me back when I was in the thick of the dance.

Of course, so much regarding the dating world is subjective and driven by opinion, and I'm fully aware that this book is no exception. However, I pray that you will understand that what I have written is rooted in God's Word, and I hope that it will help guide you as you navigate the sometimes volatile realm of relationship with the opposite sex.

I hope this resource will spur you on to glorify God in your dating relationship(s).

Often I've found that if your love life is out of whack, everything else in your universe is also out of whack. Friendships can feel off, eating habits suffer, social engagements become tainted, and even your relationship with God can be characterized by misery. I know because I've been there. It's embarrassing how many mistakes I made when I was single.

And no, I can't change history, but my desire is that you'll learn from *my* mistakes. I hope so. And if you do, perhaps your love life won't be as off-kilter as mine so often was. Maybe you'll have great godly perspective on the opposite sex, and maybe you'll make excellent dating decisions that honor Jesus and bring vibrancy, instead of anguish, to your life. Maybe you'll shine as a beacon of sanity in the insane world of dating while drawing both believers and non-believers alike to the face of Christ. Christ is the One who brings serenity in the midst of relationship pandemonium.

The dance can be amazing as you glide along smoothly to the rhythm of the music without awkwardness or injury. Sometimes, however, the dance feels more like a mosh pit: aggressive large people everywhere, and you're the little person in the middle, stepped on with every beat of the drum. Either way, it's unpredictable.

Nearly everyone will have a unique experience, but the most important thing to remember is that Jesus is with you in the process. In the Old Testament, the book of Daniel talks about three men who honored the Lord by refusing to fall down and worship an image that King Nebuchadnezzar had made. The king warned the three men (Shadrach, Meshach, and Abednego) that they would be thrown into a burning furnace if they refused to worship the golden image he had set up, and they responded collectively by telling the king that God would save them from death—*but even if He didn't,* they still wouldn't worship the king's false god (Daniel 3:18).

There are many things in this world that can lure us away from loving Jesus with all of our hearts, but none quite as powerful as the shine of romance. Many of you will date and it will lead to a lasting marriage relationship. Many of you may not. What is paramount in either situation is that we not allow our relationship status to come between us and our relationship with God. He may allow your dating life to work out—*but even if He doesn't* (Daniel 3:18), don't turn away from your first love.

There are many who have stopped following God because a romantic relationship didn't turn out the way they wanted it to. God "didn't deliver" for them in dating, or marriage, or singleness, or infertility, or whatever, so they turned away and left their relationship with Jesus on the curb. I've seen it many times, and it is heartbreaking...

As followers of Christ, each of us is called to a life of faith, and this includes the area of romance. We should live with a sense of confidence that God will provide a lasting, godly relationship for us, *but even if He doesn't*, we pledge our loyalty to follow Him because we understand that He wants what is best for us. The cost of loyalty to our Creator can sometimes be great, but a willingness to pay the price is what is asked of us. The cost for Shadrach, Meshack, and Abednego was the possibility of death, and they were willing to pay it because they believed that God knew what He was doing. We must live the same way--believing during both good times and bad that God knows exactly what He is doing when it comes to what we need.

Cling to Him in times of relationship sadness, heartache, loneliness, hurt, and confusion. Cling to Him in times of jubilation, zeal, comfort, fulfillment, and exhilaration when every detail of your dating life is humming along. We need Jesus when things are horrible and we need Jesus when things are wonderful. He is the ultimate, regardless of the state of your dating relationship.

He is the Alpha and the Omega, the beginning and the end (Revelation 22:13). He is before all things, and in Him all things hold together (Colossians 1:17). No one will ever love you the way He does. Remember this as you dance. It will make the experience worth it because regardless of the outcome, it's an experience *with Him*.

THANKS

WHEN I PITCHED THE IDEA of writing a book on dating to my friend Rick James, he looked at me intently with a furrowed brow. I tried to speak as persuasively as I could because I genuinely believe that this is an area a lot of single people need help with. When my little speech ended, I said something like, "Well, what do you think?"

Rick paused for what seemed like hours but was probably only a few seconds. And with the wrinkle in his forehead still in place, he looked me in the eye and said, "You have to write this, and I have to publish you."

I owe so much of my public influence to Rick James. We met a long time ago when I was just a wee little sophomore in college, and he has believed in my ability to communicate in ways that nobody else has, spurring on my creativity and resolve to influence others for the glory of Jesus Christ. Rick has helped me, encouraged me, cared for me, and bought more lunches for me than one man should.

I love Rick James like a brother, and I can't thank him enough for giving me yet another opportunity to make an impact in this world for God's Kingdom.

I appreciate you more than I could possibly communicate, Rick. Thank you for everything...when do you want to get lunch again? Your treat.

* * *

Thank you also to my wife, Rachael. You have always been honest with me about my writing, and I am so very thankful that you don't pull any punches. You do it because you are committed to excellence for God's glory and I love that about you. You are the most outstanding example of grace and truth I have ever known, and I'm still super confused why you picked an idiot like me to spend your life with...but I'm thankful you did.

Rachael, you are my best friend, an incredible mother, a thoughtful communicator, and a joy to be married to. Thanks for letting me date you. Let's keep dating until we get really old, die together, and go to heaven at the exact same time, holding hands. Cool? Cool.

* * *

Thank you to those who contributed to making this book a possibility. My editor, Katie James, who for the sake of excellence, hacked away at any of my sloppy writing...and did so with kindness. To Matt Smethurst, who helped me tremendously in the research process by suggesting sources I never would have been able to come up with on my own. To Andy Allan and Tom Flack, my gifted proofreaders and amazing friends.

* * *

Finally, I'd like to thank a few of the heroes of the faith who have poured into me over the years. Many of their words and ideas have shaped the way I think and communicate and have influenced some of the very things here in this book. I'm thinking specifically of Dan Flynn, Roger Hershey, Dave Broadwell, and Tim Henderson. Thank you for spending your lives pouring into other lives like mine. The world is not worthy of godly men like you.

ABOUT
THE
AUTHOR

*Shelby Abbott is a Philadelphia based author, emcee, and public speaker
on staff with the Campus Ministry of Cru. His passion for college ministry has
led him to speak at campuses all over the United States and author
the books Jacked, and I'm Awkward, You're Awkward. He has one wife (Rachael),
two daughters (Quinn and Hayden), a bulky comic book assemblage, multiple
t-shirts, and a rather impressive vinyl LP record collection.
For more information about Shelby and his ministry, including his blog, you
can visit him online at www.shelbyabbott.com.*

BIBLIOGRAPHY

1   Alex Williams, *The End of Courtship?*, (http://www.nytimes.com/2013/01/13/fashion the-end-of-courtship.html?pagewanted=all&_r=5&), accessed August 11, 2014, nytimes.com.

2   Ibid.

3   Andrew Byers, *TheoMedia: The Media of God and the Digital Age*, Cascade Books, 2013.

4   Betty Blake Churchill, *Fantasy: I Gave My Word to Stop at Third*, CruPress, 2010.

5   Marion Jordan Ellis, *Sex and the City Uncovered: Exposing the Emptiness and Healing the Hurt*, B&H Publishing Group, 2010.

6   Anna Bartlett Warner, *Jesus Loves Me*, 1860.

7   *A Few Good Men*, Directed by Rob Reiner, Columbia Pictures, 1992.

8   Ellen Fein and Sherrie Schneider, *The Rules: Time-tested Secrets for Capturing the Heart of Mr. Right*, Grand Central Publishing (Warner Books), 1995-02-14.

9   Eugene H. Peterson, *The Message*, Copyright Eugene H. Peterson, 1993-02.

10 *Dementor*, Harry Potter Wiki, (http://harrypotter.wikia.com/wiki/Dementor), accessed August 11, 2014.

11 C.S. Lewis, *The Four Loves*, Geoffrey Bles, 1960.

12 https://twitter.com/MattSmethurst, accessed August 11, 2014.

13 Marion Jordan Ellis, *Sex and the Single Christian Girl: Fighting for Purity in a Rom-Com World*, Bethany House Publishers, 2013.

14 Yolanda Wikiel, *Tangled Up In Tech*, Real Simple Magazine, January, 2014.

15 J.K. Rowling, *Harry Potter and the Goblet of Fire*, Scholastic Press, 2000.

16 *Catfish*, Urban Dictionary, (http://www.urbandictionary.com/define.php?term=catfish), accessed August 11, 2014.

17 Christopher Hudspeth, *18 Ugly Truths About Modern Dating That You Have to Deal With*, (http://thoughtcatalog.com/christopher-hudspeth/2014/04/18-ugly-truths-about-modern-dating-that-you-have-to-deal-with/h7jsDAgg7sDwQV1h.01), accessed August 11, 2014, ThoughtCatalog.com.

18 Ingrid Michaelson, Trent Dabbs, Barry Dean, *Girls Chase Boys*, 2014.